THE WAR AT HOME:
JAPAN DURING WORLD WAR II

Titles in the series include:

LUCENT LIBRARY *of* HISTORICAL ERAS

THE WAR AT HOME:
JAPAN DURING WORLD WAR II

LINDA SPENCER

LUCENT BOOKS

An imprint of Thomson Gale, a part of The Thomson Corporation

THOMSON

™

GALE

Detroit • New York • San Francisco • New Haven, Conn. • Waterville, Maine • London

© 2008 Thomson Gale, a part of The Thomson Corporation.

Thomson and Star Logo are trademarks and Gale and Lucent Books are registered trademarks used herein under license.

For more information, contact
Lucent Books
27500 Drake Rd.
Farmington Hills, MI 48331-3535
Or you can visit our Internet site at http://www.gale.com

LIBRARY OF CONGRESS CATALOGING-IN-PUBLICATION DATA

Spencer, Linda.
  The War at Home : Japan during World War II / by Linda Spencer.
    p. cm. -- (Lucent library of historical eras. Twentieth-century Japan)
  Includes bibliographical references and index.
  ISBN 978-1-4205-0027-1 (hardcover)
  1. World War, 1939-1945--Japan. I. Title.
  D767.2.S74 2007
  940.540952--dc22
                                                              2007035900

ISBN-10: 1-4205-0027-9
Printed in the United States of America

Contents

◆

Foreword

Looking back from the vantage point of the present, history can be viewed as a myriad of intertwining roads paved by human events. Some paths stand out—broad highways whose mileposts, even from a distance of centuries, are clear. The events that propelled the rise to power of Germany's Third Reich, its role in World War II, and its eventual demise, for example, are well defined and documented.

Other roads are less distinct, their route sometimes hidden from view. Modern legislatures may have developed from old tribal councils, for example, but the links between them are indistinct in places, open to discussion and interpretation.

The architecture of civilization—law, religion, art, science, and government—as well as the more everyday aspects of our culture—what we eat, what we wear—all developed along the historical roads and byways. In that progression can be traced every facet of modern life.

A broad look back along these roads reveals that many paths—though of vastly different character—seem to converge at a few critical junctions. These intersections are those great historical eras that echo over the long, steady course of human history, extending beyond the past and into the present.

These epic periods of time are the focus of Historical Eras. They shine through the mists of history like beacons, illuminated by a burst of creativity that propels events forward—so bright that we, from thousands of years away, can clearly see the chain of events leading to the present.

Each Historical Eras consists of a set of books that highlight various aspects of these major eras. For example, the Elizabethan England library features volumes on Queen Elizabeth I and her court, Elizabethan theater, the great playwrights, and everyday life in Elizabethan London.

The mini-library approach allows for the division of each era into its most significant and most interesting parts and the exploration of those parts in depth. Also, social and cultural trends as well as illustrative documents and eyewitness accounts can be prominently featured in individual volumes.

Historical Eras present a wealth of information to young readers. The lively narrative, fully documented primary and secondary source quotations, maps, photographs, sidebars, and annotated bibliographies serve as launching points for class discussion and further research.

In studying the great historical eras, students also develop a better understanding of our own times. What we learn from the past and how we apply it in the present may shape the future and may determine whether our era will be a guiding light to those traveling future roads.

Timeline

1932 Japan creates the puppet state of Manchukuo.

1937 The Marco Polo Bridge Incident sparks war between Japan and China.

The Japanese government launches the National Spiritual Mobilization Campaign.

1940 The Greater Japan Patriotic Industrial Association is formed.

The Information Board takes strict control over the news media.

Community councils are formed.

1941 The Greater Japan Youth Association is formed.

Japan's attack on Pearl Harbor starts war between Japan and the United States.

1942 Allied forces win the Battle of Midway. Japan is now on the defensive.

The Greater Japan Women's Association is formed.

1943 The Japanese government begins evacuating civilians from cities.

1944 U.S. forces begin bombing the Japanese islands.

All Japanese students age ten and older are required to work almost full time.

1945 The United States drops atomic bombs on Hiroshima and Nagasaki. The Soviet Union declares war on Japan. Japan surrenders. World War II ends.

Introduction

JAPANESE DAILY LIFE, 1930–1945

As an island nation, Japan needed to look outward for resources to support its growing industries and population. The Japanese took an aggressive stance to acquire these resources, first from China and then from other Asian nations. Japanese expansion across Asia led to conflict with the Allied powers, particularly the United States. To achieve victory in this conflict, Japan's leaders instituted a policy of total war from the 1930s until 1945.

A total war policy means that every part of society is engaged in some effort toward success in the war. This all-encompassing policy was strongly supported by the Japanese people.

Support for a total war policy arose partly because Japan saw itself as the leader of Asia. According to historian Peter Duus, as early as 1910 the "defense and maintenance of empire ... had become a basic [motto] of Japanese foreign policy. ... [The] idea that Japan was the natural leader of the Asian peoples took deep hold of the public imagination."[1] For Japan to assume this leadership position, it had to engage in an aggressive foreign policy. Japanese leaders decided to use every available resource to succeed in this effort. In other words, they chose to wage total war.

The policy of total war gained support in the 1920s and 1930s. A new generation of army leaders gained prominence in Japan and pressed for stronger Japanese action abroad. These new leaders had learned from the outcome of World War I that "modern wars were won on the home front as well as on the battle front. ... Without a total mobilization of the civilian population and more crucially, a strong and autonomous industrial base, victory would be difficult."[2]

To put the total war policy into effect, Japan needed a strong military, behind

By 1944, near the end of World War II, many homes were destroyed. On the outskirts of cities, such as Hiroshima, homeless children built fires in the street to keep warm.

which the people could rally. The military needed factories that provided weapons, ammunition, and other military supplies, including food. The factories needed raw materials, many of which Japan lacked. Japan did not have large areas of uncultivated land for agricultural expansion, either. Manchuria, on the Asian mainland, met many of Japan's needs. It had vast resources of iron, for

example, and land on which Japanese farmers could settle. Japan invaded Manchuria, marking the first step in Japan's efforts to create an empire and acquire the resources it needed.

Economic factors played a part in the popularity of the total war policy in Japan as well. In October 1929, an enormous stock-market crash in the United States signaled the beginning of a worldwide economic depression. This depression shrank the world market on which Japan had become dependent. Japanese manufacturers cut production, reduced wages, and fired employees. Small-scale merchants and agricultural workers were seriously affected. A crop failure in 1931 added to the problems.

These economic troubles led to political stress among Japanese political parties, cabinet ministers, and army leaders. Uncertainty about Japan's future increased civilian support for a new militaristic policy. Japan was reorganized to become a national defense state.

The total war policy had dire effects on the lives of the Japanese people. Japanese soldiers were trained to serve their country by any means necessary. Even when the tide of the war turned against Japan, its soldiers continued to serve the emperor, sometimes by giving their lives on suicide missions. The government rallied popular support for the war, the soldiers, and the suicide missions through a campaign carefully crafted to win the hearts and minds of the Japanese people. News reports and radio broadcasts were edited to present only the information that the government wanted people to have.

Japan's civilians supported the war effort in a variety of ways. Many provided moral support by assembling care packages for the soldiers and creating special send-off gifts, such as thousand-stitch belts and bouquets of cherry blossoms. Women went to work in factories, took care of homes, and ran family businesses. They coordinated neighborhood defense associations. Children, too, served the war effort by working in the fields or in factories. In some cases, schools were turned into factories. All civilians were expected to give everything they had in support of the war. The campaign continued until the war's last days, when leaders called upon civilians to defend their homes to the death if the Allies invaded.

The Allied invasion never happened, but the refusal of Japanese leaders to consider defeat or surrender still led to disaster. Allied firebombing campaigns destroyed Tokyo and other Japanese cities. U.S. atomic bombs devastated Hiroshima and Nagasaki. By the end of the war in 1945, nearly everyone in Japan had lost loved ones, homes, or possessions. Millions died and millions more were injured. Yet, despite the challenges and disasters they faced, the Japanese people endured.

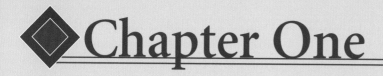

Chapter One

Japan Goes to War

For Japan, war was not a random act. Japan perceived war as the answer to its need for natural resources and a stepping-stone in its quest for global respect. Japanese leaders spent years planning wars—first with China and later with the United States. In their eyes, war was the solution to their country's problems, and success was the only possible outcome.

Japan's plan began with attacks on China in the early 1930s. From China, Japan expanded into Indochina and other parts of Southeast Asia. This expansion caused the breakdown of diplomatic and trade relations with the United States. The breakdown led to war.

Japan in China

An island nation, Japan lacked the natural resources needed to sustain an industrial economy. It had to rely on imported raw materials. The territory of Manchuria in northeastern China was rich in coal, iron ore, and oil slate. Japanese leaders had been eyeing those resources since the end of the nineteenth century. In 1905, after winning the Russo-Japanese War, Japan took control of the southern half of Manchuria. Although Japan built the South Manchurian Railroad and developed the region's economy, Chinese warlords remained the military power in the region.

In the late 1920s, when a new generation of military leaders came to power in Japan, pressure grew for a stronger Japanese presence in Manchuria. The new leaders believed, from observing World War I in Europe, that victory in modern warfare required a nation's total effort. These leaders pushed for a total mobilization of Japan's resources, including the civilian population, and the development of a strong industrial economy. With its rich raw materials and vast undeveloped agricultural lands, Manchuria met many of Japan's total war needs.

On September 18, 1931, Japanese army personnel dynamited a small part of the South Manchurian Railroad. Japanese troops stationed in Manchuria to protect the railway claimed it was the work of Chinese saboteurs and declared a state of emergency. The Chinese government, weakened by civil war, put up no resistance.

In 1932, Manchuria was renamed Manchukuo and declared an independent state. It became a Japanese puppet state with Pu'yi, the last emperor of China, as its puppet ruler. Japanese lead-

The independent state of Manchukuo, which was established in 1932, was comprised of three northeast Chinese provinces.

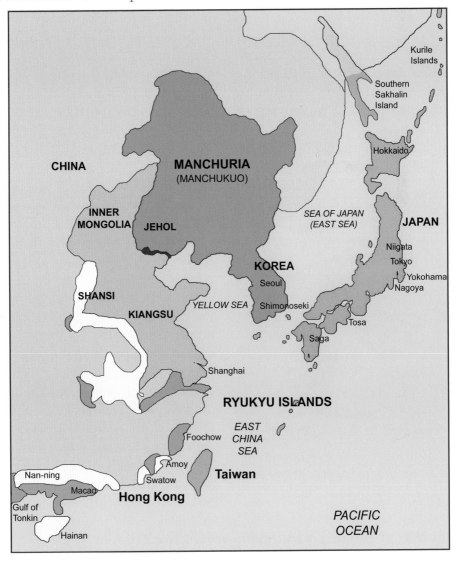

ers held key positions in the Manchukuo government, and Japan used the state as a base for further aggression in northern China. In 1932, the League of Nations, an organization of global cooperation similar to today's United Nations, called for Japanese troops to withdraw from Manchukuo. Japan responded by withdrawing from the League of Nations.

Life in Manchukuo

After the creation of Manchukuo, more than 800,000 Japanese colonists from all walks of life moved to the region. Fukushima Yoshee was one of them. She was a kindergarten teacher who went to Fushun, Manchuria. "I was so full of

In the 1930s, Japan used propaganda posters to encourage Japanese people to pursue a better life in Manchukuo.

enthusiasm," she remembers. "I wanted to do everything. I believed we have to take care of the children of Manchuria because Manchuria has been taking care of Japan. I thought I might even marry someone in Manchuria."[3]

Fukushima became sick twice while teaching in Manchukuo and both times had to return to Japan to recover. She married a Japanese shopkeeper who had started a prosperous business in Manchukuo after being discharged from the army. "We had a big house. … We had all the food we wanted—cans of bamboo shoots, dried tofu without limit, and shiitake and other mushrooms. … In Japan there was so little already. Clothing was rationed and food had begun to disappear. Simply having so much food made Manchuria attractive."[4]

War with China

The establishment of Manchukuo began a period of Japanese aggression in China. Fighting a civil war, the Nationalist Chinese government, called the Guomindang and led by Chiang Kaishek, ignored the Japanese threat. China's Communist rebels, led by Mao Zedong, did fight against the Japanese. While this action won popular support for China's Communist Party, it did not stop the advance of the Japanese military.

In 1937, the Marco Polo Bridge Incident sparked Japan's war against China. Although Japan had a newly organized government under Prime Minister Konoe Fumimaro, army officers continued to

Japanese soldiers performed a victory march through the streets of Shanghai during the Second Sino-Japanese War, which lasted from 1937 to 1945.

push for stronger action against China. On July 7, 1937, Japanese troops and Chinese troops exchanged gunfire at the Marco Polo Bridge outside of Beijing. It is unclear who shot first.

Local commanders arranged a truce, and within days, a cease-fire was in effect. The Chinese government, however, was no longer willing to tolerate Japanese aggression and sent new troops into the area. The Japanese government responded by increasing its forces. New skirmishes broke out. Japanese representatives went to Guomindang headquarters in Nanjing to discuss matters, but the conflict continued to spread. The Second Sino-Japanese War—and World War II in Asia—had begun.

On July 28, the Japanese launched a strong offensive against Chinese forces in Beijing. They bombed areas of the city, and Chinese troops withdrew. The Japanese army entered Beijing on August 4.

In the 1930s, the city of Shanghai was a cosmopolitan city with considerable Western commercial investments. In 1932, during a battle in Shanghai, the Chinese had fought the Japanese to a standstill, and Western powers had not interfered. The Japanese counted on the same lack of interference as they advanced on the city again in August 1937.

Like the Marco Polo Bridge Incident, the battle for Shanghai escalated into a major conflict that started from a suspi-

The First Sino-Japanese War

Japanese military leaders had good reason to believe that China would give them free reign in the region. Almost forty years prior to occupying Manchuria, Japan had engaged China in military conflict and won.

In the 1880s, as a response to possible Western colonization, Japan sought a line of interest, or buffer zone, in territory near its island borders. Because Korea was just across the Sea of Japan, Japanese leaders believed that Japan's security depended on keeping Korea free of control by any other nation.

In a series of political schemes, Japan supported one faction of Korea's unstable government and China supported the other. Matters culminated in 1894 with a peoples' rebellion in southern Korea. China sent troops to stop the rebellion; Japan sent a larger force. The Japanese military seized the royal palace and forced the king into an agreement that gave the Japanese the right to expel the Chinese. Ill-equipped and poorly trained, Chinese troops were no match for the Japanese. China's Qing government negotiated a peace settlement within a few months. China recognized Korea's independence and gave Taiwan and the Pescadores Islands to Japan.

cious situation. A Japanese marine attempted to illegally enter a Chinese military airport in Shanghai, possibly encouraged by Japanese militants to spark an incident. Chinese police killed the marine. Japan sent troop reinforcements to Shanghai. China sent troops to the city as well.

Within days, Chinese and Japanese forces in the area were engaged in open warfare. The battle of Shanghai was one of the bloodiest in the Second Sino-Japanese War. It lasted until the end of November, when Chinese troops, overmatched by the well-equipped and well-trained Japanese army, withdrew. After winning Shanghai, the Japanese army turned its attention to Nanjing, China's capital.

Chinese military leaders announced that they would fight to the death to defend Nanjing, but the chaos that followed their defeat at Shanghai resulted in a quick Japanese victory. The Chinese government abandoned Nanjing and moved south to Chongqing. Japanese soldiers went on a house-to-house search for Chinese soldiers, which became a rampage of killing and looting. The brutality of the Japanese soldiers in Nanjing has prompted some historians to claim that this behavior "will stain forever the honor of the Imperial Army."[5]

While moving the government from

This Japanese propaganda photo shows Chinese children celebrating the occupation of China by Japan during the 1930s.

Nanjing to Chongqing, Chiang Kaishek and the Nationalists adopted a scorched-earth policy. This meant that they destroyed anything that could be useful to the advancing Japanese army, including food crops and buildings that might be used as shelters. They destroyed dams and levees to flood the land and make it more difficult to cross.

The Japanese committed about 700,000 soldiers to the war with China. Japan maintained control of the area around Beijing, main railway lines, and major coastal cities, such as Shanghai, but land forces could not launch a successful offensive through the interior. In addition, Japanese-controlled territories were subjected to guerrilla-style attacks, espe-cially in the north, where the Communists had bases of support. A guerrilla attack is a style of warfare used by small groups against larger armies. It usually involves quick attacks on soldiers or supplies. Despite early victories, the Japanese army was hindered by the guerrilla warfare used by the Chinese Communists. Within two years, Japan was bogged down in the war in China.

Red Canisters

The Japanese military used any means necessary to clear residents out of China's villages and cities. In some cases, soldiers committed brutal acts of violence against the civilians they encountered. In other cases, they used poison gas to drive people out, even though the use of poison gas had been made illegal after World War I.

The gas was meant to be a more efficient, less personal means of clearing out a population. No hand-to-hand combat or eye-to-eye contact was required. Tanisuga Shizuo, a gas soldier in the Japanese army, explained, "[U]sually if you attacked an enemy position frontally, you had to take them at bayonet point. With gas, they'd just run. It was easy. Funny to use that word, but it was true."[6]

Each squad kept a supply of two or three red canisters containing the gas. The gas was released from the canister by lighting a fuse. The burning fuse would release the gas in the form of smoke. After lighting the fuse, a soldier threw the canister as far as he could. Tanisuga could throw his canisters about 55 yards (50m).

Because the gas turned into smoke, wind was an important factor. If it changed direction, the soldiers might end up gassing themselves. Learning to determine the best conditions for using gas was part of becoming a gas soldier. For Tanisuga, "the best time to use it was immediately before a rainstorm, when air pressure was low and the wind was blowing slowly and steadily in the direction of the enemy. I learned how to measure wind speed as part of my training."[7]

According to Tanisuga, the Japanese used poison gas in China throughout the war but kept it secret. Soldiers were required to collect the used canisters and other pieces of evidence from the battlefield. Official military announcements listed cities that were captured but never stated that gas was used in the captures. Because newscasts were censored, Japanese civilians knew little about the use of gas or any other aspect of the war.

Japan in Southeast Asia

In November 1938, Japan's leader, Prime Minister Konoe, announced his "vision of a New Order in East Asia."[8] Konoe linked the purpose of the Sino-Japanese War with defeat of Western powers, such as Great Britain and the United States. The New Order was supposed to be based on cooperation among China, Japan, and Manchukuo. All three of these nations, Konoe said, had been excluded from their place in the world by Western powers and the Western puppet, Chiang Kaishek. As leader of China's Nationalist government, Kaishek worked very closely with Western countries, including the United States. Konoe and China's Communist Party saw this close relationship as a betrayal.

Japanese aggression in Southeast Asia was the next step toward Konoe's New Order. By 1940, Japanese leaders planned to benefit from the war in Europe. As the Germans conquered French and Dutch colonial nations in Europe, the Japanese looked to take over French and Dutch colonies in Southeast Asia.

In the summer of 1940, Japan's foreign minister announced a new part of Japan's foreign policy, the Greater East Asia Co-Prosperity Sphere. The sphere was meant to be an alliance of Asian nations with Japan as its leader. The allied nations would provide labor and resources to strengthen Japan's economy. According to Japanese propaganda, the sphere was nothing like European colonialism. In reality, it was hard to tell the difference. Pursuit of this policy put Japan in conflict with the United States, which had its own economic interests in the region. As Japan pushed farther into Southeast Asia, relations with the United States worsened.

President Franklin D. Roosevelt, limited by popular opinion in the United States, could not aid China or the countries of Southeast Asia against Japanese aggression, but he could act in other ways. Roosevelt saw Japan's actions as part of a larger global problem: disrespect shown by some nations for the laws and independence of other nations. In October 1937, Roosevelt gave his Quarantine Speech, in which he urged people to stop this "epidemic of world lawlessness."[9]

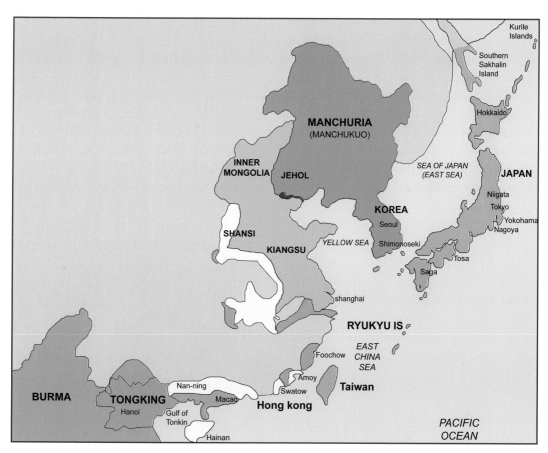

The Japanese army controlled many areas in the Pacific during World War II. This map shows where the Japanese territory expanded during the war.

In addition, Roosevelt adopted a policy of U.S. economic sanctions meant to force Japan to abandon its aggression in China and Southeast Asia. By the mid-1930s, one-third of all Japanese imports came from the United States. Many of these imports were important to Japan's military. In the summer of 1938, Roosevelt imposed a "moral embargo [prohibition of trade]" on shipments of aircraft, weapons, and other war material to Japan. In July 1939, the United States cancelled its commercial treaty with Japan. In the summer of 1940, Roosevelt restricted the exportation of airplane fuel, scrap iron, and steel to Japan after the Japanese built airfields in French Indochina. In July 1941, after Japan assumed control of all of French Indochina, Roosevelt froze Japanese financial assets in the United States and imposed an oil embargo. Great Britain and the Netherlands followed. Japan lost 90 percent of its oil imports.

There wasn't any chance at all that the Dutch governor general of the East Indies was going to agree to sell us oil … the American embargo on oil sales to Japan would have become meaningless, so the American consul general was right on top of events. … But I guess even we who were there didn't fully realize that at the time. 'Somehow things will work out for Japan'—that's what we thought. That's because Japan saw itself as so strong.[10]

By September 1941, Germany had already conquered much of Europe and was at war with Great Britain. Japan joined the European war in name only by signing the Axis Pact with Germany and Italy. The goal of the pact was to keep the United States out of the war in Europe and the war in the Pacific.

The oil embargoes against Japan by the United States, Britain, and the Nether-

Getting Oil

Despite losing access to oil from the West, Japanese leaders remained positive that Japan would prevail in Asia. Yoshida Toshio, a naval officer, was sent to Indonesia to buy oil:

Tojo Hideki was prime minister of Japan from 1941 to 1944. After World War II, he was convicted as a war criminal and executed by the Allies in 1948.

Did President Roosevelt Push Japan to Attack Pearl Harbor?

World War II ended in 1945, but debate about the 1941 Japanese attack on Pearl Harbor continues. One side believes that Roosevelt provoked Japan to attack so that he had a reason to go to war. According to this perspective, Roosevelt sought to overcome the powerful U.S. isolationist movement, which wanted the United States to stay out of wars in Europe and Asia. Despite German aggression in Europe, approximately 80 percent of the U.S. population supported the isolationist movement in 1940 and 1941. To gain support for U.S. involvement in the war against Germany, Roosevelt had to counter that strong public opinion.

In 2000, a secret memo written by Lieutenant Commander Arthur McCollum, a naval intelligence officer, was obtained through the U.S. Freedom of Information Act. The memo suggested eight actions, including an embargo on all trade with Japan, meant to provoke Japan to attack the United States. Such an attack would not only start a war between the two countries but also make the American people angry enough to want to fight. Because Japan had joined Italy and Germany as an Axis power, the United States would be drawn into the European war as well. Roosevelt would be able to join the fight against Germany's leader, Adolf Hitler.

lands were meant to stop Japanese aggression in Asia and the Pacific. Instead, the policies had the opposite effect. Japanese military leaders in the government promoted open hostilities against the three nations imposing the oil embargo. The embargoes "fed the notion among military and naval chiefs that Japan should go to war quickly before its capacity to fight dwindled away."[11] Refusing to believe that oil reserves would run out, members of an imperial conference decided in October 1941 to go to war against the United States, Great Britain, and the Netherlands by the end of the year. Prime Minister Konoe resigned. Tojo Hideki, the war minister and an army hard-liner, became prime minister. Japan was on its way to war with the United States.

New prime minister Tojo began his term of office by submitting a list of demands to the U.S. government. The list included U.S. recognition of Japan's right to do whatever it wanted in China and the end of the three-nation oil embargo. The United States refused the demands, and Japan declared war.

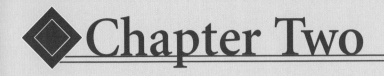

Chapter Two

The Emperor's Warriors

On Sunday morning, December 7, 1941, Japanese bombers suddenly struck the U.S. military base in Hawaii. Within two hours, a second wave of planes struck. The attack resulted in more than 4,500 U.S. casualties. The U.S. military lost 177 planes. Eight battleships were sunk or damaged, three destroyers were crippled, and three light cruisers were damaged. Japan lost 20 aircraft. The goal of Japanese war strategists was to strike quickly. They wanted to force the larger and stronger United States to the bargaining table before it could mobilize its military resources.

Several hours later, Japan's declaration of war was announced to the Japanese people. A government official read the declaration over the radio. Japanese leaders held Great Britain and the United States responsible for the war. They claimed that the support of China by Allied nations disturbed the balance of power in Asia. The Japanese called the conflict the Greater East Asia War.

The war declaration was an announcement of a total war mobilization effort throughout Japan. Young men were called to serve in the military, and civilians were called to do everything in their power to support the troops. Japanese military leaders trained their soldiers to fight to the end, and at first, victories came quickly. Each victory brought more territory under Japanese control. The military became spread thin across various Asian countries. Japan lost the ability to keep its soldiers supplied with war necessities. As a result, Japan's early military successes were followed by multiple defeats.

Released in 1970, Tora, Tora, Tora *was the first major motion picture to show the attack on Pearl Harbor from the perspective of both the Japanese and the Americans.*

Becoming a Soldier

By 1941, the Japanese army had been fighting in China for four years. It was a well-trained and modern army consisting of two levels—officers and common soldiers. The officers were a privileged group of men who had been educated at Japan's military academies. Common soldiers were drafted mostly from the lower classes of people, especially the farming population.

According to military affairs clerk Debun Shigenobu, Japan "could raise large-scale units [of soldiers] in less than twenty-four hours."[12] A tightly organized group of government employees ran the draft. The country was divided into conscription, or draft, districts. A draft is the calling up of civilians for required service in the military. Each town had a military affairs clerk, such as Debun, who handled conscription and kept detailed records on draft-eligible men. At age twenty, all males had to report for a conscription exam. After soldiers had served their active duty, they could still be called until they reached the age of forty. When the war turned against Japan after the Battle of Midway in 1942, both younger and older men were drafted.

Recruits were considered expendable. Army draftees were often called *issen gorin*, which meant "one *sen*, five *rin*"—or less than a penny—which was the cost of the draft notice postcard that recruits received. A secret monitoring system recorded when a draft-eligible male moved, attended school, changed jobs, and even when he married and had chil-dren. This information was gained in a variety of ways. According to Debun, "I often walked around in the village to learn what the villagers were up to. Even those walks belonged to the realm of military secrets."[13] The way in which soldiers were called up was secretive too. Debun explains:

> Most of the time, notifications came in the middle of the night. An envelope was delivered to the village police chief from military headquarters. … I would open it in the presence of the mayor. Until that moment, even I didn't know who was going to be drafted. … All this was to prevent spying. The mustering of soldiers was a military secret….[Y]ou didn't want to give the enemy information about how many soldiers Japan was calling up or where they were assembling.[14]

Once drafted, soldiers endured harsh training. The functioning of the Japanese army depended on the absolute obedience of its soldiers. To learn unquestioning obedience, recruits went through a system of rigid discipline, beatings, and harassment. Recruits were to consider each order, no matter what it was, as coming from the emperor himself. It was instilled in recruits that anything necessary to achieve total victory for the emperor was permissible. The soldiers, relieved of all personal responsibility, were not afraid of consequences. Some historians see a link between these sol-

Japanese soldiers were trained to do whatever was necessary to achieve victory in war. Soldiers took this training to heart during the Japanese invasion of the Philippines in 1941.

diers and the samurai, who went into battle unafraid of death. Both followed the ethic known in Japan as *Bushido*—the "way of the warrior"—an "absolute loyalty and unhesitating sacrifice."[15]

A Soldier's Life

Even in the early war years, when Japan was fighting only China, a soldier's life was brutal. Suzuki Murio, a well-known poet in Japan, fought in China in 1939. He remembers that "if you didn't move along with the main force when you were out in the countryside, there was always the possibility you'd be captured. Everyone was scared of that. We were all exhausted."[16]

As European governments fell to German control in 1940, Japan invaded European colonies in southern and southeastern Asia. Before long, many Japanese soldiers were serving their nation in countries far from their homeland. Suzuki remembers, "In March 1942, we knew we were about to be sent to the Southern Area because we were wearing summer uniforms in the midst of the falling snow. We shipped out. … [T]hey spread out a map of the Philippines, so for the first time I knew where we were headed. … In the Philippines, the enemy showed himself to us."[17]

Fighting in the Philippines was brutal. Suzuki continues:

By the time we approached the front line, we were already exhausted. "Fall out!" they said, and you'd collapse for five or six minutes. Lie down and try to catch your breath. In the dark you can't see well, but there was a horrible stench. I threw myself down on what turned out to be the belly of a dead horse. … Later that night we were given another short rest, but it was such agony to get up once you'd sat down that I tried to sleep standing up.[18]

Despite the terrible conditions, Japanese soldiers did not rebel, but obeyed and fought—often until death.

The Greater East Asia Co-Prosperity Sphere

Japan had announced in 1940 its intent to form a Greater East Asia Co-Prosperity Sphere. After Pearl Harbor, Japan continued to strike swiftly throughout the Pacific. By early 1942, Japan had expanded its control over a large part of Asia. Its forces captured Singapore, the Philippines, Indonesia, and several Pacific islands, such as Guam. The Japanese even had a small foothold in the Aleutian Islands, near Alaska. The Greater East Asia Co-Prosperity Sphere eventually included the Asian countries Japan had invaded and now administrated: Manchuria (Manchukuo), the Dutch East Indies (Indonesia), Indochina, Thailand, the Philippines, Burma, and eastern China.

Japanese propaganda declared that the Greater East Asia Co-Prosperity Sphere

Emperor Hirohito

Hirohito became the emperor of Japan in 1926 at the age of twenty-five. His reign, known as the Showa era, was a turbulent period in Japanese history. Today, many historians acknowledge that Hirohito remains an ambiguous figure in twentieth-century history. They are reexamining his role in leading Japan to war and his knowledge of the attack on Pearl Harbor.

Herbert P. Bix, in *Hirohito and the Making of Modern Japan*, points out that U.S. policy was to depict Hirohito as a powerless emperor who had no control over Japan's military or the decision to go to war. This interpretation worked to the advantage of the Allied occupation forces. After the war, Hirohito provided a much-needed point of national unity in Japan. To many Japanese, Hirohito was the godlike embodiment of Japan. General Douglas MacArthur, leader of the Allied occupation forces, knew this and saw to it that Hirohito was not tried for war crimes. In return, Hirohito cooperated

with MacArthur in remaking Japan along American guidelines.

The fact remains, however, that the Japanese cabinet made the decision to go to war in Hirohito's presence, and he was kept fully informed of military plans.

Hirohito became emperor in 1926, when he was 25 years old. He became the 124th emperor in a direct family line spanning more than 2,600 years.

would liberate Asian countries from Western control. Under Japanese rule, Asia would be for Asians, and Asian countries would control their own destinies. At first, Japanese forces received enthusiastic greetings when they arrived. Within hours after the attack on Pearl Harbor, for example, the government of

Map showing territories included in the Greater East Asia Co-Prosperity Sphere.

Thailand granted Japan permission to use Thai air bases to invade British-held Burma and the Malay Peninsula. A month later, Thailand declared war against Great Britain and the United States. Burmese leaders who opposed Western imperialism, or the taking of colonies, organized the Burma Independence Army to march with the Japanese army as they invaded Rangoon, the capital of Burma, in 1942. Soon, however, leaders of nations in the Co-Prosperity Sphere learned something that the Koreans and Chinese already knew—that Japanese colonists could be as exploitative and brutal as Western colonists had been. In many cases, life under Japanese administration proved to be even harsher than life under Western imperialism.

Belonging to Japan's Greater East Asia Co-Prosperity Sphere meant that a nation's natural resources and labor force belonged to the Japanese total war effort. For the most part, the Japanese military administered nations within the sphere and strictly controlled local economies to acquire essential materials for Japan. Troops supervised trade and transport to Japan of important resources such as petroleum, rubber, tin, and rice. Before Japan created the sphere, it had imported these goods. Now it simply took them. In this way, control of other Asian nations allowed Japan to achieve economic self-sufficiency.

Hundreds of thousands of people living in the nations of the Co-Prosperity Sphere were recruited, lured, or simply forced into labor service battalions (groups). These workers built roads, airstrips, or railroad lines in other countries. Given barely enough to eat, no medical care, and subject to brutal discipline, many laborers died far from their homes.

Japanese forces stationed in sphere nations lived off the land and relied on local supplies of food. The military commandeered what they needed from the local people and demanded delivery of supplies. They paid in a military currency that lost value as the war progressed. Local people faced chronic shortages of food and other basic goods. On the Malay Peninsula, for example, the Japanese army allotted native populations only one-half the rice ration, or portion, the Japanese received. Anyone caught stealing from military warehouses was beheaded.

Army soldiers and civilian administrators stationed in sphere nations brought with them a deep sense of Japan's superiority. They imposed a system of Japanization in each place. People were to bow to all Japanese in military uniform. Everyone had to observe Japanese holidays, such as the emperor's birthday. Even the calendar changed. The year 1942 became the year 2602—counted from the supposed founding of the imperial state of Japan in 660 BCE. Japanese officials closed many local schools and converted them into army barracks, or accommodations for soldiers. In schools that remained open, Japanese was a mandatory subject.

Local populations received harsh treatment. Soldiers, trained to believe in Japanese racial superiority, had low opinions of those who were not Japanese. Consequently, they treated the native people inhumanely, slapping, beating, and verbally berating them. Violence was routine in sphere nations. In Indonesia, residents could be executed for listening to Allied broadcasts on shortwave radio. When Japanese soldiers captured Singapore, they arrested more than seventy thousand Chinese residents. Accused of rebellious activities, thousands of these Chinese were tied together, put onto boats, taken to the middle of the harbor, and pushed overboard.

Women especially suffered in the Greater East Asia Co-Prosperity Sphere. Thinking they had signed up to work overseas in textile plants, women were sent to work for Japanese soldiers and colonial administrators instead. Chinese, Filipino, Malaysian, Dutch, and Korean women were forced into labor. Tens of thousands died from disease and malnutrition. Near the end of the war, the Japanese shot many of them.

Administering Indonesia

A major part of Japan's vision for the Greater East Asia Co-Prosperity Sphere was the Dutch East Indies, or Indonesia. Indonesia was a large petroleum producer, so Japan, which did not have enough petroleum resources of its own, needed to tightly control it. The Japanese army and navy each had a geographic section of the country to administer.

Nogi Harumichi was part of the naval Civil Administration Department for the province of Celebes in Indonesia. He describes how the Japanese administration of Indonesia progressed:

In 1942 I thought occupying a country was a wonderful thing. When our ship arrived at the Celebes, in Indonesia, I saw wide stretches of uncultivated soil. "We can develop this land and introduce Japanese technology here, I thought. …The Japanese were being treated as liberators… [T]his lasted through the end of 1942. Then the military demanded an allotment of the rice harvest. … [T]here was tension among the locals and troops had to be mobilized to control it.[19]

As the Allies gained more victories, the tide of the war turned. Nogi remembers, "[A]mong the Japanese forces themselves the atmosphere became more and more brutal. Violent incidents occurred regularly. … The Indonesian people knew, thanks to their illegal short-wave radios

The belief that Japan could be the cultural and political leader of Asia, free from Western powers, began in the late 1800s. By the end of 1942, the Japanese army had invaded several Asian countries, including the Philippines, Malaya, and Burma.

Training Japanese Officers

All Japanese officers passed through the military academy at Ichigaya. Most who attended this academy had been cadets at military preparatory schools. At Ichigaya, officer trainees lived in simple quarters and were cut off from their families. The following is a typical daily schedule:

Officers in training at the Ichigaya Military Academy.

5:30 A.M. Reveille [Sounding of a bugle to awaken soldiers]
6:30 A.M. Breakfast
7:00–8:50 A.M. Private study
9:00–11:50 A.M. Lectures
NOON Lunch
1:00–4:00 P.M. Gymnastics, fencing, jujitsu, equitation (horseback riding), drill, and lectures on the training manual
4:00–5:00 P.M. Free exercise
5:00–6:00 P.M. Private study
6:00 P.M. Supper
7:00–8:20 P.M. Private study
8:30 P.M. Roll call
9:00 P.M. Lights out[1]

[1] Meirion and Susie Harries, *Soldiers of the Sun: The Rise and Fall of the Imperial Japanese Army* (New York: Random House, 1991), 171–172.

that Japan was losing. … Just listening to short wave—well that was enough reason to execute them. It was in military law and was accepted."[20]

The Tide Turns

While Japan conquered much of the Pacific swiftly and easily, administering its newly acquired empire proved difficult. The military effort required a flow of raw materials from the conquered lands. Getting conquered people of different cultures to work for Japan's total war effort required highly skilled administrators. Japanese leaders could not meet either requirement. The result was an increasingly dire lack of raw materials and personnel.

Once the United States focused resources on its own war effort, it outstripped Japan in military production, personnel, and air and naval power. The first significant defeat for Japan, the Battle of Midway in June 1942, occurred only six months after the attack on Pearl Harbor. The Japanese planned to lure the U.S. Navy into a surprise battle in which Japan would destroy the aircraft carriers that had survived Pearl Harbor. The U.S. military learned of the plan and was able to prevent it from being implemented. Instead, the United States attacked the Japanese fleet near the islands of Midway, sinking four aircraft carriers and damaging other ships. As one historian explained, "[I]n a stroke, Japan's supremacy on the high seas and in the air was shattered, and its strategic plans started to unravel as military initiative shifted to the United States."[21] For the first time, Japan was on the defensive, an outcome for which its military leaders had not prepared.

Gyokusai

The huge losses at the Battle of Midway stopped Japan's military progress. Japanese leaders, however, never really came to grips with Japan's "altered strategic situation."[22] The Allies had a series of quick victories, and by the summer of 1944, they were at Saipan, only 1,000 miles (1,609km) from Japan. Japanese soldiers throughout the Greater East Asia Co-Prosperity Sphere found themselves under Allied attack.

The decision of Japanese leaders to place military forces throughout the sphere had overextended Japan's ability to assist its troops. Logistical support of forces in the Co-Prosperity Sphere nations collapsed. Soldiers found themselves without military supplies and unable to live off the land. This lack of support for its troops was one of the major failures of the Japanese war plan.

As the Allies advanced with their well-kept and well-supplied armies, evacuation of Japanese troops was impossible. Furthermore, moving from one area to another would expose the abandoned area to Allied attack. Faced with what they considered two unacceptable options, Japanese military leaders chose a third option: to "stand in place and die."[23]

Japanese troops were encouraged to fight to the death rather than surrender. Soldiers and civilians were told that it was better to die courageously than to give up, even if they knew they would not survive the battle. This concept was known as *gyokusai*.

One person who lived through the war describes gyokusai as "the 'crushing of jewels,' meaning people giving up their

lives joyfully for their country rather than succumbing to the enemy or falling into their hands."[24] Gyokusai meant that Japanese soldiers, trained into total obedience and often starving, exhausted, and sometimes even weaponless, would charge the enemy until they were killed. The Allies called these Japanese suicide attacks *banzai* charges. "Banzai" was part of a cry used by Japanese soldiers that meant "Long live the emperor!"

Japan's leaders described these suicidal attacks to civilians only in positive terms and praised the soldiers for their "splendors of honorable death and faithful service."[25] Gyokusai, or the spirit of *tokko* (special attack), glorified death and suffering. As the Allies approached Japan's home islands, Japanese leaders told soldiers and citizens not to falter and assured them that there was honor in personal destruction.

Saipan

After their victory at Midway, the Allies concentrated on a drive across the Pacific using a strategy called island hopping. They advanced toward Japan by conquering one island at a time. In July 1944, the United States captured the Japanese-held island of Saipan. Part of the Northern Mariana Islands, Saipan occupied a strategically important location approximately 1,000 miles (1,609km) southeast of Japan. The Japanese had controlled the Northern Mariana Islands since 1920.

In 1945, Japanese soldiers in Korea marched south to obtain transport home.

On June 15, 1944, 535 American ships carrying 127,570 troops attacked the island of Saipan. During the 24 days of the battle, more than 43,000 Japanese soldiers were killed.

After the Allies captured Saipan, they were close enough to fly B-29 bombers over the main islands of Japan.

Yamauchi Takeo was one of three survivors from a company of 250 soldiers who fought on the island of Saipan. More than 43,000 Japanese soldiers died defending the area. He reached Saipan on May 19, 1944:

The impression I had when I landed was that they had made no preparations for defense at all. ... I was eating a large rice ball when I heard a voice call out, "The American battle fleet is here!" I looked up and saw the sea completely black with them. What looked like a large city had suddenly appeared offshore. ... Japanese soldiers really accepted the idea that they must eventually die. If you were taken alive as a prisoner you could never face your family.[26]

Despite this belief, Yamauchi surrendered to U.S. forces on July 14 and was held as a prisoner of war in LaCrosse, Wisconsin.

The B-29s were more advanced than the Allied bombers being used in Europe at the time. They could carry a full bomb load for more than 3,000 miles (4,828 km) at a faster speed than the older bombers. In November 1944, using B-29s from air bases on Saipan, Allied forces began to bomb Japanese cities.

The Lily Corps of Okinawa

The Battle of Okinawa, which began on April 1, 1945, was the beginning of the official battle for the Japanese home islands. It is an example of how effectively soldiers and civilians practiced tokko. Okinawa lies at the southernmost point of Japan's forty-seven prefectures. (A Japanese prefecture is similar to a U.S. state or a Canadian province.) Civilians on Okinawa had already begun preparing for battle in early 1945. In mid-February, an Okinawa newspaper urged "all residents ... exhibit your tokko spirit."[27]

Students at the island's high school and middle schools were called to serve in a student corps. Girls served in the Himeyuri Student Corps, or Lily Corps, working in hospitals to care for the wounded. As Miyagi Kikuko, a former member of the student corps relates, at their quickly arranged graduation ceremony, they sang a song that encouraged them to "give your life for the sake of the Emperor, wherever you may go."[28] Hospitals were set up in caves scattered around the town. As the U.S. military rained bullets and bombs on Okinawa, the number of wounded overwhelmed the students. Miyagi remembers, "Those [soldiers] who had gotten into the caves weren't so lucky either. Their turn to have their dressing changed came only once every week or two. So pus would squirt in our faces, and they'd be infested with maggots. Removing those was our job."[29]

Miyagi recalls a horrendous march to another part of the island while under constant bombardment. "The road ... was truly horrible, muddy and full of artillery craters with corpses, swollen two or three times normal size, floating in them. We could only move at night."[30] She left the cave with nineteen people—three teachers and sixteen students. By the time they were captured by the Americans, only one teacher and eleven students were still alive.

When the Americans announced over bullhorns that they were there to help, Miyagi "thought we were hearing the voices of demons. From the time we'd been children, we'd only been educated

The Himeyuri Corps was made up of schoolgirls between the ages of 15 and 19 years old. More than 200 of these girls died during the Battle of Okinawa.

to hate them."[31] The Americans sent the students to Kunagami Camp in the north of Okinawa. Eventually, Miyagi was reunited with her family.

The Cherry Blossom League

Japan's war ideology (beliefs) of glorified suicide led to the formation of the *tokkotai*, which stood for the Divine Wind Special Attack Corps. The corps was a Japanese suicide force that struck Allied ships in the last year of World War II. The Allied forces called these soldiers *kamikaze*, a Japanese word that means "divine wind."

As the Allies continued to make gains, the Japanese government increased its efforts to portray suicide as a worthy, heroic choice for military and civilian populations during wartime. Vice Admiral Onishi Takijro, a naval officer, developed the tokkotai. Onishi and his officers "thought that the Japanese soul, which was believed to uniquely possess the strength to face death without hesitation, was the only means available for the Japanese to bring about a miracle and save their homeland."[32] Unable to face the reality of losing the war, Japanese leaders resorted to a plan based on a kind of superstitious thinking that enough deaths in battle would somehow save their nation.

Tokkotai attacks were basically a denial of the inevitable Japanese defeat. The Divine Wind Special Attack Corps used airplanes, gliders, and submarine torpedo-like navy vessels. Eventually, tokkotai included any attack on the enemy from which the attacker did not return. None of the plans developed for this corps provided any means for soldiers to return to base.

To enhance and further beautify the imagery of death, the government used the cherry blossom as a symbol for the tokkotai air corps. A single cherry blossom was painted on both sides of each plane, and officials used various Japanese words for cherry blossoms to name divisions of the corps. Cherry blossoms were in full bloom in the spring of 1945 when the suicide attacks intensified. Many tokkotai pilots flew off with branches of cherry blossoms attached to their helmets and uniforms.

There were about four thousand tokkotai pilots, of whom about three thousand were young boys drawn from newly drafted and enlisted soldiers. About one thousand were university students who graduated early to be included in the draft.

Japanese propaganda claimed that tokkotai pilots volunteered for their assignments. In fact, a combination of military obedience training and peer pressure played a large role in the young men's decisions to volunteer for the Divine Wind Special Attack Corps. Sometimes commanding officers called a division of the corps to a large hall where they reminded recruits of their duty to Japan. Then they told each corps member to declare in front of everyone whether he volunteered or not. Such pressure was difficult to counter. Araki Shigeko, the

It is believed that around 7,000 kamikaze pilots died during World War II.

bride of a corps pilot, recounts her husband's experience: "One night, he came home suddenly, without any warning. … He told us he'd been given permission to take overnight leave. … He told us he'd been selected as a group leader of a Tokko mission. … 'When can I see you again?' I asked. He said only 'I'll be back when it rains.' … All of us waited for him whenever it rained."[33]

Kamikaze Diaries

Several tokkotai pilots left behind diaries. These documents are testimonies to the young men's struggles to meet others' expectations and to find meaning in a death they "felt was decreed for them."[34]

Hayashi Tadao attended the Imperial University of Kyoto and was drafted as a student soldier on December 9, 1943. He wrote in his diary in January 1944:

I don't care what happens any more. The most painful and unbearable feeling comes from this life of forced indifference, a life in which we bump into a brick wall even as we walk one step. … The hard part is not death, but to live. At the height of life, life is terminated, the curtain goes down. Maybe it is splendid. After the climax the messenger of death arrives without notice. This is a splendid scenario. But, it is unbearably miserable.[35]

Nakao Takenori graduated from the

University of Tokyo with a law degree. He was drafted as a student soldier in December 1943. He died on a tokkotai mission in May 1945 at age twenty-two. Before his suicide mission, he wrote his parents, "I can now meet my death with the belief that I have been treated with sincerity by people when I have not done anything for them. … Although I did not do much in my life, I am content that I fulfilled my wish to live a pure life, leaving nothing ugly behind me."[36]

The pilots who flew these missions had been born and raised in a culture that was constantly preparing for or fighting a war. They knew only the militaristic Japan, one in which every aspect of daily life was devoted to a total war existence.

Cherry Blossoms and Japan

Cherry blossoms, called *sakura* in Japanese, and the annual spring blooming have long been a favorite event in Japan. As far back as the eighth century, the Japanese performed a special ritual for the fertility of the earth under the flowering cherry trees. More than fifty varieties of cherry blossoms cover the entire Japanese archipelago, or group of islands, each spring. The blooming is often marked by traditional celebrations in which people dance, sing, participate in poetry and calligraphy competitions, and feast under the blossoms.

The cherry blossom had been used as a military symbol since the 1920s. Near the end of World War II, the flower became the symbol of the tokkotai corps. School and popular songs, textbooks, films, and plays all linked the cherry blossom to military service. The fact that the flower is a beautiful blossom with a short life span made it an apt symbol for the young pilots of the tokkotai corps.

In 1912, Japanese officials gave thousands of cherry trees to the city of Washington, D.C., as a gesture of friendship. The trees were planted around Washington's Tidal Basin. Each spring, the city holds its Cherry Blossom Festival.

In Japan, cherry blossoms are a symbol of a life lived to the fullest. Because their flowers are so beautiful, but only bloom for a short time, they are associated with warriors who have died in battle.

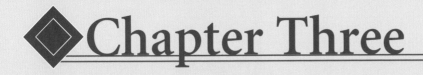

Chapter Three

Promoting Loyalty

The total war effort in Japan during World War II required the cooperation and support of every member of society. The Japanese government promoted the war effort even when defeat seemed certain. Through carefully crafted campaigns in newspapers, magazines, cartoons, films, paintings, music, dance, and poetry, leaders sought to win the hearts and minds of the Japanese people. The goal was to maintain public support for the emperor and the government no matter how badly the conflict was going. Unaware that the Allies were winning, the Japanese people remained committed to the war effort even though they suffered severe hardships.

One Hundred Million Hearts Beating as One

During World War II, Japanese leaders used imagery to encourage people to support the war effort. Because the government controlled the media, it was possible to spread that imagery throughout the nation. One popular slogan described the image of one hundred million hearts beating as one human bullet to defeat the enemy. Imagery such as this increased national pride, united the population, and kept the public loyal to Emperor Hirohito.

The national political organization of Japan was called *kokutai*. In the early years of Hirohito's reign, political and military leaders debated the policy of kokutai, stressing that it should include the best possible principles. For many leaders, kokutai revolved around two important ideas of the Japanese state. One was that a divine line of emperors had ruled from the beginning of time. The other was that family-like ties united the "benevolent sovereign with his subjects."[37] The 1890 Imperial Rescript on Education supported this vision of kokutai.

FREEDOM

NIPPO

RISONERS AT ZENTSUJI

WHERE FREEDOM REIGNS

The PICTORIAL ORIENT

Price 70 Sen

Vol. IX, No. 8

AUGUST, 19

8

No 2
第二期

攝影新聞
PHOTO-NEWS

ATTLE OF HONGKONG

WAR PICTURES 50 CENTS
伍角

Imperial Rescript

The Imperial Rescript was an edict (declaration) on education issued in 1890 by Emperor Meiji, who ruled Japan from 1866 to 1912. It was supposed to guide the education of schoolchildren and be a moral compass for Japanese society. The rescript called for obedience to the emperor. As part of the total war effort, students had to memorize the rescript and recite it each morning in school.

The rescript states: "Our Imperial Ancestors have founded Our Empire on a basis broad and everlasting" and calls upon the emperor's subjects to "offer yourselves courageously to the State; and thus guard and maintain the prosperity of Our Imperial Throne coeval [contemporary] with heaven and earth."[1]

The rescript further instructs: "[B]e Our good and faithful subjects, [and] render illustrious the best traditions of your forefathers. The way here set forth is indeed the teaching bequeathed by Our Imperial Ancestors, to be observed alike by Their Descendants and the subjects . . . ."[2]

[1]"Imperial Rescript on Education," Meiji Shrine (Meiji Jingu), http://www.meijijingu.or.jp/english/intro/education/index.htm (Accessed May 14, 2007).
[2]Ibid.

As a result of this debate, a new nationalism developed under Hirohito that incorporated the rescript and became known as *kodo* (the imperial way). One historian explains, "The 'imperial way' was a motivating political theology [religious belief] sprung from the idea of the emperor as the literally living embodiment of Japan past and present, a paradigm [model] of moral excellence all should follow."[38] Kodo united Japan and helped create a unique Japanese identity. As part of kodo, the Japanese people

Japanese propaganda was meant to garner civilian support for the war effort.

rejected the ideas of other civilizations, such as individualism, communism, and Western democracy. Instead, they embraced the emperor-centered state as the focus of their national identity.

A Test of Loyalty

Loyalty to the state was severely tested when Allied powers bombarded Japan near the end of the war. The bombardment made every aspect of daily life challenging. Yet when the people first learned how bleak the outlook really was for Japan, their loyalty did not falter. Young Japanese women jumped off cliffs rather than surrender to Allied forces on the island of Saipan. The government presented this information to the public as evidence of the glory of civilian sacrifice. In reporting the story, one newspaper quoted a professor at Tokyo Imperial University as saying that "our courage will be buoyed up by this one hundred times, one thousand times." The professor further encouraged readers to "sacrifice before our great victory."[39]

The great victory to which the professor referred was the mistaken belief held by many Japanese that Japan could still win the war. Japanese leaders told the citizens of Japan that because the United States was a nation of individualists, the U.S. government had to fight a short war in order to keep the American pacifist (peace) movement under control. The propaganda spread throughout Japan: if the Japanese refused to surrender, the Americans would tire of fighting, and the United States would pull out of the war.

Many citizens of the United States had indeed favored peace and isolation during the early years of World War II. After the Japanese attack on Pearl Harbor, however, most Americans wanted to join the conflict. Japan's leaders seriously underestimated the commitment of U.S. civilians to the war effort as well as the strength of the U.S. military. They continued to encourage Japanese civilians to make supreme sacrifices, assuring them that Japan would win the war.

To further strengthen home-front loyalty, the Japanese government launched a campaign using civic groups, publishing organizations, and the film and music industries to promote the war effort. In 1940, Prime Minister Konoe had formed two national associations. The Imperial Rule Assistance Association brought together citizens' groups, labor groups, and arts groups. The Greater Japan Patriotic Industrial Association brought factory workers into one large group.

The Greater Japan Youth Association was established in January 1941. It merged four youth councils that had originated in the 1920s. By 1942, the youth association had built its membership by expanding to include young people from ages ten to twenty-five. Membership in the youth association grew from just over four million to nearly fifteen million young people. Local youth clubs were expected to "drum home the aims of the war and to marshal [organize] work teams to perform spot jobs in neighborhoods and on the farms."[40]

Dozens of private women's groups had formed prior to World War II to promote such issues as suffrage, consumer rights, and birth control. In February 1942, these organizations were all combined into the Greater Japan Women's Association. The goal of this reorganization was vague. One Japanese newspaper explained that "its main purpose is to make good mothers."[41] By all accounts, during the war, Japanese women remained loyal to the state, the emperor, and their families.

Overall, the Imperial Rule Assistance Association was too cumbersome to be effective. By mid-1942, it was nearly useless. The basic strengths of the associations for factory workers, young people, and women, however, remained effective at the local factory and neighborhood levels throughout the war.

Controlling Words

Books, films, and music were included in the government's campaign to ensure loyalty. In December 1940, the Cabinet Information Bureau was renamed the Information Board. The Information Board had strict control of the press, the book trade, broadcasting, and the film industry. The Japan Publishers' Council, a group of Japanese book publishers, found that their paper and ink supplies became scarce if they did not work with the Information Board. In 1943, the Japan Publishers' Association replaced the Publishers' Council. The association reduced the number of publishers from more than 3,000 to only 204.

Few books of original, free thought were written and published during this time. Many writers served in the military or worked in factories. This meant they did not have the time to write about their reflections. Some were sent to the battlefront specifically to gather material to write about the success of the war. Any writer who wrote a book not requested by the Information Board had to find a publisher with the supplies and means to publish it. Most writers cooperated with the war effort. Many joined the Japan Patriotic Literary Association formed by the Information Board in May 1942. This association sponsored such patriotic works as *The Tradition of Loyalist Thought*

and *The History of the Japanese Spirit*.

Movies and Music

Members of the film industry worked with the government as well. After 1940, the Information Board sponsored films to raise the morale of the people. In March 1942, officials gave film producers explicit rules to follow. Films had to "promote national policy and strengthen people's feelings against the enemy."[42] As paper was rationed to publishers, so film was rationed to filmmakers. Newsreels showed military successes that would stir audiences, such as *The Battles of Hawaii and Malaya of 1942*, which included scenes of Japanese planes attacking U.S. ships at Pearl Harbor. Footage of Japanese soldiers in Japan's new southern empire and naval parachute units descending into battle helped convince people that the war effort was successful.

Music played an important role in films and on the radio. It helped maintain a mood of pride and loyalty in Japanese daily life. Composers were told to produce patriotic works within the Japanese classical tradition. Radio stations were told to broadcast marches and war songs continuously.

The government used slogans on posters, on the radio, and in newspapers to remind people to sacrifice for the nation and emperor. Such slogans as "Luxury is the enemy," "Deny one's self and serve the nation," and even "Serve the nation with one death" were widely circulated. The total war effort influenced

I Loved American Movies

Despite escalating tensions between Japan and the United States in the late 1930s and early 1940s, American movies played in Japanese theaters. Screenwriter and director Hirosawa Ei recalls American films he saw before war broke out. "I loved the American movie. ... I became a fan of Gary Cooper. I saw his *Beau Geste, Dawn Patrol,* and *Morocco.* ... In *Farewell to Arms,* I couldn't understand why Cooper tore off his military shoulder patches from his uniform, and escaped. ...The hero who dies for the nation ... became images of heroism to me."[1]

In 1941, before Pearl Harbor, Hollywood studios decided to close their offices in Japan. Hirosawa remembers, "I felt desolate,

thinking I wouldn't be able to see American movies anymore."[2] The images of America as presented through the films remained with Hirosawa, however. "Those American and British movies really formed my mental character ... I remember the day the war started against America and England. I was still a middle-school student. ... I didn't think war with America and Britain would ever come. They were great nations for which I was filled with respect."[3]

[1]Haruko Taya Cook and Theodore F. Cook, *Japan at War: An Oral History* (New York: The New Press, 1992), 242.
[2]Ibid., 243.
[3]Ibid., 244.

and controlled every aspect of Japanese life.

Painting War Art

The Japanese government controlled painters just as it controlled writers and filmmakers. Maruki Iri and Maruki Toshi remember that painters were "forced to paint pictures that supported the war. Unless you drew war paintings, you couldn't eat."[43]

Painters who refused to paint war pictures could not get any art supplies. Those whose paintings showed the war

in a positive way "received money, paints, brushes. All the things they needed."[44]

Young painters were drafted into the military as soon as they finished art school. They were told to paint images of victorious battles for the military. Some artists who refused were imprisoned and lived in horrific circumstances in prison. Those who could not hold up "might end up painting pictures of the annihilation of America and Britain."[45]

Maruki Toshi sums up most artists' decision to paint war pictures or not: "Painters always want to paint something. If they ordered you to paint, most painters probably would, even war painting."[46]

She reflects about painter Fujita Tsuguji, who painted for the military. According to Toshi, "[Fujita] was such a brilliant painter that if you look at his *The Day of Honorable Death on Saipan*, you can almost imagine this is a painting opposing the war. The truth comes out, presses forward in the picture. … His war paintings show the misery of war. It seeps out."[47]

A Holy War

Propaganda in the form of cartoons and posters greatly contributed to the total war effort in Japan. Japanese propaganda spoke of Japanese superiority and reflected the view that the Japanese were the most advanced race on the planet.

Given that Japan was a member of the Axis powers with European nations Germany and Italy, the Japanese government tended to downplay antiwhite interpretations of the war. Official statements outlining Japanese superiority to the "barbaric" enemy did not discourage antiwhite sentiments among the people, the media, and the military, however. Soldiers sent to Indochina were given the booklet *Read This and the War is Won*. The booklet specifically identified the enemy as white Europeans and Americans. Propaganda leaflets written in Chinese and air-dropped in China stated that "to liberate Asia from the white man's prison is the natural duty of every Asiatic!"[48]

Cartoons depicted the West as a beast with claws, fangs, animal hindquarters, and sometimes a tail or small horns. These features indicated a demon, an evil spirit, or a monster. In fact, the dominant metaphor in Japanese propaganda against the West was that of a devil.

The creators of Japanese propaganda made the enemy into a devil or an evil spirit and then presented the war as a "holy war for the establishment of eternal world peace."[49] According to the propaganda, this world peace could be traced back to the founding of the Japanese state more than three thousand years ago. Including this lineage allowed propaganda officials to stress the divine origins of the Japanese imperial line and, by association, the Japanese people.

According to the propaganda, this divine heritage was both a blessing and a vulnerable legacy. The goal of the war was to restore racial and spiritual purity lost in recent times as Western culture and values had spread across the world. The Japanese people were taught to believe that the sacrifices they made to wage war in Asia purified both themselves and their country. All were to participate in this process, not just soldiers. The greatest sacrifice a person could make for emperor and nation was the supreme sacrifice of life itself.

News of the Day

Beginning in late 1940, the Japanese government attempted to control information in the news media about the total war effort. They rationed paper and forced journalists to join writers' federations and follow government guidelines in reporting. News was generally slanted in favor of the government.

As part of the total war effort, the Japanese government imposed strict control on the news media by forming the Information Board in December 1940. In 1941, the government created the Newspaper League, which controlled the amount of paper that newspaper publishers received. The Newspaper League followed instructions from the Information Board. If the board disliked stories in a particular newspaper, that publisher received less paper on which to print editions. After the Newspaper League began to manage paper distribution, the number of daily newspapers in Japan shrank from 454 to 54 in only two years.

After the attack on Pearl Harbor in December 1941, the Information Board told news publishers which stories they could report. The news now had to be written in close cooperation with the government. To ensure that cooperation, officials restructured the Newspaper League in February 1942 to form the Newspaper Council. This council wielded even more power, including the power to revoke the membership of any reporter whose views its leaders disliked. This made it virtually impossible for the reporter to find another job.

The Japanese government formed the Patriotic Publicists Association in December 1942. Members included journalists, technical writers, and public relations people. The association's purpose was to "take the lead in the empire's external and internal ideological warfare."[50]

Managing Magazines

The Information Board censored weekly and monthly magazines in Japan as well as newspapers. Officials required magazine publishers to join the Japan Publishers' Cultural Association. The association distributed paper and monitored magazine content. The government required magazine editors to submit the names of their writers to the association before printing magazine articles. As with newspapers, the number of weekly and monthly magazines dropped.

In September 1942, the government replaced top editors at two of the largest Japanese monthly magazines, *Chuo Koron* and *Kazo*. Officials arrested fifty-nine people associated with *Chuo Koron* and other publications for allegedly organizing a secret plot to revive the outlawed Japanese Communist Party. Some of these people died in prison from the torture they received. That same week, the senior staff at *Kazo* was fired for printing a historical article that the Japanese police considered untruthful. Both magazines managed to keep publishing until mid-1944, when the government suddenly closed them. In response to the resulting controversy, Prime Minister Tojo is quoted as saying, "The masses are foolish. If we tell them the facts, morale will collapse."[51]

Newsreels

In addition to newspapers and magazines, the government disseminated news through newsreels shown at movie theaters. Asai Tatsuzo filmed battles for Domei News Agency, which made the newsreels. He remembers, "[B]ack home, people were desperate for news from the front. They formed long lines to get into the news movie theaters that showed only newsreels, just war, but it was all 'Banzai, Banzai!'—just emotion."[52]

Asai went to every Japanese battlefront for nine years, from the China Incident in 1937 to the surrender in 1945. Of all the footage he sent back, the agency used only film that showed Japanese success-es. Asai says, "I flew to New Guinea. I saw planes hit around me. I didn't really film our planes going down, though. Only once, a plane in our formation catching fire and going down wreathed in flames."[53]

How Asai handled this footage of a Japanese plane crashing conveys just how tightly the government regulated what news reached the public and what news was kept secret. According to Asai, "I sent that film in separately, about a hundred feet of it, wrapped in red tape, indicating it was secret. I was told it was forwarded to the air office of the Munitions Ministry, where it was used for research into where our planes caught fire."[54]

The Emperor's Voice

On August 15, 1945, Emperor Hirohito announced over the radio that the war was over. Days before, on August 9, the Soviet Union had entered the war against Japan and moved quickly into Manchuria. Faced with this new threat in addition to the atomic destruction of Hiroshima and Nagasaki, Japanese leaders were forced at last to abandon their policy of no surrender.

The emperor never used the words *defeat* or *surrender* in his announcement, however. Instead, he said that the war had not "developed to Japan's advantage."[1] He urged his people to "endure the unendurable and suffer what is insufferable."[2] The Japanese people had never heard Hirohito's voice until that day. A government official had announced the beginning of the war in 1941.

A resident of Tokyo recorded in his diary, "All of us sank into silence and didn't say a word. I felt in a daze, exasperated ... I keenly felt a sense of cruel grief."[3]

The defeat destroyed the myth that Japan's mission was to build a new Asian order. It shattered the ideal that war was positive or ennobling.

[1]Quoted in Peter Duus, *Modern Japan*, 2nd ed. (Boston: Houghton Mifflin, 1998), 248.
[2]Ibid.
[3]Ibid.

Asai survived the war. After the Domei News Agency disbanded during the U.S. occupation of Japan, Asai worked for the U.S. Signal Corps. He was assigned to film the war crimes trials in Tokyo. He thought the trials were victors' justice and noted that there was not even a mention of the atomic bombs. As Asai learned, however, after years of working under state-controlled media, "the news reports shouldn't reflect your feelings. People who watch the news should reach their own conclusions about what's going on. That's the way it should be, isn't it?"[55]

Despite Asai's theory, the people of Japan were not allowed to draw their own conclusions about the war. Every piece of information they received about the conflict was carefully crafted to present the total war effort as noble and successful. Even as the realities of war overwhelmed the daily life of Japan's civilian population, the information campaign relentlessly continued.

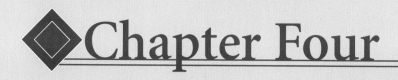

Chapter Four

The War at Home

Japanese women, children, and elderly men who stayed at home during the war did not directly join the fighting, but they were still an important part of Japan's war effort. They provided support and encouragement to soldiers by writing letters and sending care packages. In addition, they supplied the labor necessary to maintain daily life. Later, many worked outside the home in agriculture and in factories.

As the war continued, women and children became more vital to Japan's labor and defense forces. Officials turned schools into factories where students worked on secret projects for the military. Japanese civilians of all ages were taught and encouraged to defend themselves and their homes from the approaching U.S. forces. Like Japan's soldiers, civilians were asked to sacrifice their lives to save their country. As the situation became more desperate, those on the home front suffered further hardships as a result of their leaders' quest for total victory.

Women, Work, and the War

Before the war, Japanese women often joined the workforce after they finished their schooling. When they married, usually by the age of twenty-five, women were expected to give up their jobs. A married woman could continue to work only if it did not interfere with her traditional duties as a wife and mother. Many married women helped on family farms or in family businesses. According to demographer Irene B. Taeuber, even after the war began, "the major contribution of women remained the unpaid toil of the married women who assisted their husbands in field, shop, or house."[56] With the escalation of the war, however, women's roles began to change.

Women in Tokyo helped clean up debris after the city was bombed during the war.

By 1941, the government required all young, unmarried women to register for possible work. Nevertheless, Japanese leaders remained reluctant to encourage women to work, even when there was a labor shortage. Prime Minister Tojo expressed the state's attitude toward women—particularly married women—working outside the home for the war effort when he said: "That warm fountainhead which protects the household, assures responsibility for rearing children, and causes women, children, brothers, and sisters to act as support for the front lines is based on the family system. This is the natural mission of the women in our empire and must be preserved far into the future."[57]

Historians estimate that three million women, including hundreds of thousands of middle school girls, made up a large part of the workforce by the end of the war. This figure represents only 10 percent of Japan's female population at that time. However, these numbers do not account for all the extra duties women took on at home. In some cases, married women stepped in to take over their husbands' shops and businesses without formally joining the workforce. Arakawa Hiroyo, who owned a cake shop in Tokyo with her husband, described the war's effect on local businesses:

As the war grew hotter, many people we dealt with were called up to the front or drafted for labor service. … It didn't seem to happen all at once, but soon you'd notice: "The man of that house is gone," or "He's been taken away for labor." Many shops and businesses closed or were left in the hands of women.[58]

Women assumed community responsibilities that expanded their roles beyond wife, mother, and homemaker. They became involved in the National Defense Women's Association, community councils, and neighborhood associations. According to Arakawa, "once you joined, you had to go out all the time, and couldn't do anything in your own place."[59]

The Faith and Trust of a Thousand Women

Government leaders wanted women to remain in their traditional roles. At the same time, they needed women to help with the war effort. To achieve this goal, the government launched the National Spiritual Mobilization Campaign in 1937. The campaign united Japan's existing patriotic organizations under a single umbrella. The National Defense Women's Association was included under this umbrella. At first, joining the National Defense Women's Association and other patriotic groups was voluntary. Later in the war, membership became required.

Members of the National Defense Women's Association performed various duties to support the military. They prepared care packages for troops at the front and wrote them encouraging letters. They made *senninbari*, the thousand-stitch belts that soldiers usually wore under their uniforms when they went into battle. These belts were considered charms to protect soldiers from injury and death. To make senninbari, women stood on street corners and asked each woman who passed by to make one stitch on the belt. They did this until they had collected one thousand stitches, which symbolized the trust and faith of one thousand Japanese women.

In addition, the government launched various campaigns of conservation and sacrifice. One campaign encouraged women to wear *monpe*, or utilitarian pants, instead of traditional kimonos. This was due in part to the limited availability of cloth. Kimonos used more fabric than pants. Other campaigns encouraged women to go without fancy clothes, Western fashions, and Western hairstyles, such as permanent waves.

The Kimono

Kimonos are colorful traditional robes worn by Japanese women and men as far back as the eighth century. Some historians say that the kimono is based on a type of Chinese robe. At various times throughout Japan's history, the kimono has defined the social and economic status of the wearer. The more elegant and complex a kimono was, the higher the social status of the person who wore it.

The basic kimono is an ankle-length gown with long sleeves that are very wide at the cuffs. There are no buttons or ties. The right side of the kimono wraps around the body and then overlaps with the left side. A broad sash called an *obi* secures the kimono at the waist.

In the late nineteenth century, women began to work outside their homes. Because kimonos were not practical to work in, women began to wear other clothes. Today, most Japanese women own at least one kimono, however, which they wear for a coming-of-age ceremony on their nineteenth birthday. In rural Japan and on some of the smaller islands,

community elders still wear the traditional gowns. People wear kimonos at weddings as well, but they usually rent the garments.

During the period between the First and Second World Wars, the Japanese government promoted the conservation of materials for use in the military. This meant that kimono designs became less complex.

Working in Collective Harmony

In September 1940, more than a year before the attack on Pearl Harbor, the Japanese Home Ministry issued Order No. 17, Essentials of Providing for Community Councils. Order No. 17 was

another governmental effort to involve all citizens in the war effort. The order explained the need for community councils, and it established the structure for organizing neighborhood associations. Community councils were regional groups meant to organize and unify people morally and spiritually. They put national policies into effect at the community level. Community councils oversaw a number of neighborhood associations.

An urban neighborhood association might consist of ten or fifteen households that were close to one another. A man who was too old for military service or factory work usually led the association. Women made up the general membership, however, and carried out the association's duties. In Tokyo, for example, neighborhood associations had eight duties, which included cooperating with community councils, preventing crime, and acting as social groups. With some variations, these remained the main activities of neighborhood associations until Japan's surrender in 1945.

As the war escalated, neighborhood associations took on more tasks. In October 1942, the national government gave the neighborhood associations the essential task of distributing all food and clothing. In May 1944, *Asahi*, the leading Japanese newspaper, reported on the women who helped run the neighborhood associations: "Recently everything from the distribution of cotton thread, socks, and toilet paper to repairing shoes, umbrellas, and pots and pans is being carried out by the neighborhood associations. … Since the captains have many occupations and places of work, there are many cases in which women do their duties for them."[60]

In addition to the distribution of goods, neighborhood associations assu-med duties of air and fire defense, becoming Japan's main line of civilian air defense by the summer of 1944. Association members held relay drills and checked that every home had sand, buckets, shovels, brooms, ladders, and cisterns (water containers) for firefighting. They wore iron air-raid helmets and dug trenches in their yards and neighborhoods for refuge during bombardments.

Neighborhood associations met formally once a month. On meeting days, the government radio station, NHK, broadcast a thirty-minute program specifically for the associations. Groups met at a member's house, with at least one person from each household in attendance. Members discussed the national war aims and worked out schedules for neighborhood duties, such as patrolling at night, cleaning gutters, and selling savings bonds.

Government leaders emphasized that people in neighborhood associations should work together voluntarily in their endeavors. Tokyo's *A Guidebook for Neighborhood Association Meetings* stated that "individual competition … should be subordinated to collective harmony."[61]

Neighborhood associations were self-sustaining. No one was paid for any work, and the associations absorbed whatever costs arose. In 1941, national officials ordered local officials to pay some of the costs of the associations. Given wartime conditions, however, this order was impossible to carry out.

The last year of the war severely test-

During World War II, the government made everyone join neighborhood associations to help with the war effort. In 1940, one group learned how to use gas masks at the Tokyo Garrison hospital.

ed the associations. Members tried to maintain some social structure and organization during the chaos of the Allied bombings. For the most part, the associations held together. They were an important part of maintaining a sense of order and continuity during the last months of the war.

The War on Childhood

Just as the war changed women's lives, it changed the lives of Japanese children. The war affected their daily school routines and what they learned. Many children were sent away from their homes to live and work. For the most part, during World War II, the lives of Japanese children ages seven and older involved nationalistic, or patriotic, schooling and labor for the war effort. Students' patriotism was reflected in their joy at the news of Japanese victories. Itabashi Koshu was in middle school in 1941 and remembers hearing of the successful attack on Pearl Harbor:

> The sound of the announcement on the radio still reverberates in my ears. "News special. News special" high-pitched and rapid. ... I felt as if my blood boiled and my flesh quivered. The whole nation bubbled over, excited and inspired. "We really did it! Incredible! Wonderful!" That's the way it felt then.[62]

Learning to Support the War

Since the nineteenth century, the Japanese national government regulated schools and controlled curricula. All children were required to attend school from first through sixth grade. There was no kindergarten. Boys and girls went to separate schools. Only privileged male students, such as sons of government officials, usually attended upper grades, which consisted of five years of high school.

When World War II began, schools taught more than just reading, writing, and math. They became places where students learned to become more patriotic and to support the military. Grade schools were renamed national schools. Textbooks were rewritten. One first-grade textbook of the time begins with the words "Forward March, Forward March, Soldiers, Forward March."[63]

In May 1937, Japanese schoolchildren received a new textbook titled *Kokutai no bongi*, which means *The Fundamentals of the National Polity*. The book stressed the superiority of Japan and its people over all other nations and emphasized the importance of family, home, and ancestors. The book presented the emperor as a military ruler and "a living god who rules our country in accordance with the benevolent wishes of his imperial founder and his other imperial ancestors."[64]

In the early years of the war, students had to undergo more physical training. They participated in martial sports, such as judo and kendo, rather than baseball. Military training was a requirement for boys in upper elementary grades and secondary school.

Working for the War Effort

As the war progressed, classroom time was shortened so students could perform school labor service. At first, such work included neighborhood or community projects such as cleaning streets or parks, gathering charcoal, or picking up leaves. These were jobs that were no longer performed by adults, who had become soldiers or factory workers.

In 1939, the government established special youth schools. Attendance at these schools was mandatory for students between the ages of twelve and nineteen who chose not to stay in school after sixth

The Japanese government eliminated summer vacation, and replaced it with the "summer training period," which taught children patriotism and love for Japan.

grade. These youth schools met at night so that students could work during the day. Classes included Japanese history and ethics, military training for boys, and home economics for girls.

As the war progressed, student workloads increased. After June 1943, labor service became a larger requirement for students past the third grade. Schoolchildren began to work more than they studied. Ando Masako, a junior high school teacher in Nagoya, remembered taking her class to the countryside to cultivate new fields in the autumn of 1943: "All 600 pupils or so from the school cut down thick weeds and pulled out rocks and tree stumps. This severe work went on for thirteen days. … I was so tired that my hoe dropped, and I forgot whether all this had any effect in the war zone."[65]

By April 1944, the government required all students older than ten to work nearly full time in the fields or war plants. Schools were turned into factories where

Internment Camps

Civilians in Japan were not the only Japanese who suffered hardships during the war. For more than 110,000 Japanese Americans in the United States, the war meant being rounded up and sent off to internment, or prison, camps meant to separate them from the rest of the American population.

The cities of San Francisco, California, and Bainbridge, Washington, had large Japanese American populations. Newspapers in each city had different opinions about the internment policy.

The *San Francisco News* called internment an "inconvenience" that was a necessary and patriotic hardship. It called upon Japanese Americans to "recognize the necessity of clearing the coastal combat areas of all possible [traitors] and saboteurs. Inasmuch as the presence of enemy agents cannot be detected readily when these areas are thronged by Japanese the only course left is to remove all persons of that race for the duration of the war."[1]

The *Bainbridge Review* saw internment as racist: "[T]here is danger of a blind, wild, hysterical hatred of all persons who can trace ancestry to Japan. ... [W]ho can say that the big majority of our Japanese Americans are not loyal [?]... [T]heir record bespeaks nothing but loyalty: their sons are in our army."[2]

[1]"Their Best Way to Show Loyalty (March 6, 1942)," *San Francisco News*, Internment of San Francisco Japanese, The Virtual Museum of the City of San Francisco, http://www.sfmuseum.org/hist8/editorial1.html (accessed April 2, 2007).

[2]Quoted in Luke Colasurdo, "The Internment of Japanese Americans as reported by Seattle Area Weekly Newspapers," Seattle Civil Rights and Labor History Project, http://depts.washington.edu/civilr/news_colasurdo.htm (accessed April 2, 2007).

Japanese internment camps were located in remote areas of Utah, Arizona, Colorado, Idaho, Wyoming, and California.

students worked to make supplies for the military. The army used Tanaka Tetsuko's school in 1944 to make a secret weapon. An officer told students that the weapon "would have a great impact on the war. [The army officer] didn't say then that we were to be making balloon bombs, only that somehow what we made would fly to America. What a sense of mission we had. … We really believed we were doing secret work, so I didn't talk about this even at home."[66]

Making balloon bombs, or rather balloons to carry bombs, was difficult. Students created the balloons by pasting sheets of paper to large boards. The paste did not always dry. At Tanaka's school, they tried to dry the boards by lighting a hibachi (a small barbeque) in the classroom. As a result, Tanaka explained, "we practically started a bonfire in the class. … Sometimes you almost got poisoned by the carbon monoxide."[67]

All in all, more than 9,000 balloon bombs were created by Tanaka's schoolmates and others throughout Japan. These balloon bombs sailed over the Pacific Ocean and about 1,000 of them reached North America. The bombs inflicted little damage and some even failed to explode.

Evacuation to the Countryside

By 1943, the government started to move people out of urban areas if they were not needed in the war plants. Many mothers with small children, as well as elderly people and the infirm (people in poor health), evacuated Japan's large cities for the countryside.

In June 1944, Allied forces began targeted bombing attacks on industrial sites near Japan's major cities. At the end of that month, the Japanese government issued a plan called *The Outline for Encouraging the Evacuation of Schoolchildren*. This plan involved the forced removal of thousands of young schoolchildren from families who lived in cities. The children were sent to group resettlement centers in the countryside. About 450,000 schoolchildren were separated from their families and evacuated to the countryside.

Students continued their schooling in their new locations, but they had demanding labor duties too. Classes rarely lasted more than an hour or two each day. Students spent most of their time outside, gathering food for the group or helping on nearby farms. They traded wheat plants, cut rice plants, placed topsoil in rice paddies, mowed weeds, and cultivated new fields, among other tasks.

Life for students was weary and depressing. Nearly all were homesick. Many lost weight from the combination of hard physical labor and poor diet. Students interviewed after the war acknowledged that "the only memory that lingered …

Even after they were sent to the countryside, children worked for the war effort by pounding rice to be made into rice cakes for the soldiers.

was searching for edible weeds or eating boiled licorice greens, bracken ferns or potato sprouts thinned by farmers."[68] The Allied bombings that had led to the children's evacuation soon intensified in an even deadlier manner.

Living Targets

The first Allied bombing of Japan was in 1942. It is often called the Doolittle Raid, because an American named Jimmy Doolittle planned and led it. The raid was more of a strategy to boost Allied morale than the start of a continuous bombing program.

When the Allies renewed bombing attacks in 1944, they dropped precision, or targeted, bombs aimed at factories. In March 1945, the Allies changed from precision bombs aimed at military targets to incendiary bombs aimed at Japanese cities. Incendiary bombs are sometimes called firebombs because they are designed to ignite fires that burn the target and the area around it. From March until the Japanese surrender in August of that year, these firebombs brought misery and hardship to the civilians who remained in the cities.

Fire from the Sky

On March 9, 1945, Allied bombers flew over Tokyo and dropped 2,000 tons (1,814t) of incendiary bombs. About

One Bomb Is Not Like Another

In World War II, the Allies used three types of bombs: conventional bombs made with TNT (dynamite); incendiary bombs, or firebombs, made with napalm; and atomic bombs made with uranium or plutonium.

The military generally categorizes the use of bombs in two ways: tactical and strategic. Tactical bombing strikes military targets, such as war ships or supply trains traveling to the battlefront. Strategic bombing strikes targets that could aid the military, such as factories, railway bridges, and city centers. The goal is to eliminate the ability to continue the war effort. The Allies' strategy in Japan used conventional bombs and strategic bombing for most of the war.

In World War II, incendiary bombing was a kind of strategic bombing that used napalm bombs. Napalm is gasoline in jelly form. When incendiary bombs hit the ground, the napalm spreads quickly and causes tremendous fires. In March 1945, the Allies began dropping incendiary bombs on Japanese cities. Except for the attack on Pearl Harbor, Japan never was able to bomb U.S. cities.

one-quarter of the city was burned to rubble. Although wartime statistics are sketchy, it is estimated that the bombing of Tokyo left more than eighty-three thousand people dead, forty thousand injured, and more than one million homeless. One historian points out that "it was the most destructive air attack in history up to that time."[69]

Thousands of people burned to death or suffocated because fires consumed so much oxygen. Many jumped into canals and rivers to escape the flames, only to drown. Neighborhood associations had tried to supply each household with fire-fighting equipment, including brooms and buckets. Such primitive equipment, however, was no match for the power of incendiary bombs.

One survivor of the March 9 bombing, a sixth grader who had returned to Tokyo from evacuation in the countryside, remembers, "When we went out, we could see that to the west, … everything was bright red. The north wind was incredibly strong. The drone of the planes was an overwhelming roar, shaking earth and sky. Everywhere, incendiary bombs were falling."[70]

On March 9, 1945, 334 American airplanes flew over Tokyo dropping firebombs. Around 80,000 people were killed.

By the end of the war, bombed-out towns in Okinawa prefecture were nearly deserted.

The Allies carpet bombed Japanese cities. Carpet bombing involves striking cities with firebombs in a pattern that will cause the greatest possible devastation. There was no letup in the raids. This strategy was designed to discourage the Japanese people and force Japan into an unconditional surrender. From March 9 until Japan's surrender in August, every major Japanese city except Kyoto was systematically firebombed.

By the end of the war, at least 20 percent of all housing in Japan had been destroyed. Survivors faced many hardships. Shelter was scarce or nonexistent. In bombed-out cities, there was no water, gas, or electric service for days. Food was scarce too. Those who had money bought food on the black market. Arakawa Hiroyo's house burned in the March 9 raid on Tokyo. She and her family "were able to dig up some rice bowls and other household things that we could still use. We also dug out a mixing bowl we'd had, almost as big as a washtub, and brought that back. We used to take baths in it. Everybody was suffering from food shortages. I exchanged kimonos for rice."[71]

Survivors deserted cities that had been reduced to rubble. Sometimes families were separated. More than ten million people fled to the countryside. About three million people left Tokyo in the weeks after the March 9 bombings. In the bombed-over sections of Tokyo, even stray dogs disappeared. Either they had been eaten or they had starved to death.

Keeping the Spirit

Even during the horror of daily bombings, Japanese people continued to support the war effort. Neighborhood associations still functioned. Since 1931, nearly every aspect of Japanese daily life had been organized with the goal of winning the war. Despite people's suffering, the bonds they felt to emperor and nation, so carefully cultivated by the government, held.

Some people stayed calm by clinging to superstitions. Some people thought that eating pickled plums or red beans with rice—all foodstuffs that were scarce—would keep them safe from harm. These beliefs gave them some comfort during the downpour of Allied bombs and its aftermath.

Despite the reality of almost certain defeat, Japanese leaders prepared for a decisive battle for the homeland. They expected U.S. forces to invade the Japanese home islands later that year. Leaders reasoned that resisting the invasion would force the United States to abandon its insistence on Japan's unconditional surrender. *The People's Handbook of Combat Resistance*, published by the government, taught civilians how to attack Americans with bamboo spears, "hatchets, sickles, hooks or cleavers or to aim karate kicks at their stomachs."[72]

In the end, such hand-to-hand combat was unnecessary. Instead of invading Japan, U.S. forces dropped two atomic bombs. The bombs did more than destroy the cities of Hiroshima and Nagasaki. The devastation they caused, and the unconditional surrender that followed, destroyed the spirit that the Japanese had been able to maintain throughout the war.

Near the end of the war, most Japanese men were away, fighting. This meant that young children had to work in factories to make supplies for the soldiers.

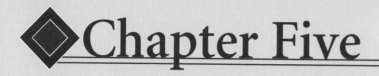

Chapter Five

The Atomic Bombs

In the early spring of 1945, the United States initiated a series of firebomb raids designed to demoralize, or damage the spirit of, Japan's civilian population. Meanwhile, scientists in the United States worked in secret to build a nuclear bomb—a bomb in which the splitting of an atom controls the explosion. This type of bomb is often called an atomic bomb. Leaders in the United States worried that German scientists would develop a nuclear bomb before U.S. scientists could. By the time Germany surrendered in May 1945, however, it was clear that German scientists had made little progress in their nuclear research.

Japanese officials, meanwhile, refused to surrender and asked civilians to fight to the end, even with sharpened bamboo sticks. The inability of Japanese leaders to accept the idea of defeat had disastrous consequences for Japan's people. Leaders in the United States decided to use the atomic bomb against Japan. The political and economic considerations behind the decision to drop these bombs were complex.

In August 1945, the United States dropped two atomic bombs on Japan. Both were dropped on civilian (nonmilitary) targets: the first on the city of Hiroshima and the second on the city of Nagasaki. The resulting devastation finally forced Japanese leaders to surrender. Hostilities ceased immediately, and the surrender became official on September 2, 1945. Japan's total war policy had been defeated, but not until it had caused severe suffering and hardship for the Japanese people.

Technology and Targets

In October 1941, President Franklin

Roosevelt authorized a group of scientists in the United States to explore the possibility of developing an atomic bomb. As early as 1939, noted physicist Albert Einstein had alerted the president in a letter that Nazi scientists were working on a nuclear weapon. If the Germans could make such a weapon, the consequences would be dire. In response, Roosevelt appointed General Leslie R. Groves to be director of a top secret project, which came to be known as the Manhattan Project.

In 1942, a breakthrough occurred on the Manhattan Project. Nobel Prize–winning physicist Enrico Fermi produced a nuclear chain reaction. The fission, or splitting, of the nuclei of uranium atoms released neutrons. The free neutrons of these split atoms hit other atoms and split them, which released more neutrons. This continuous process, called a chain reaction, meant that an atomic bomb would be much more powerful than conventional bombs.

Groves recruited physicist J. Robert Oppenheimer to lead a team of scientists to develop a bomb that would use the same kind of chain reaction that Fermi had produced. Oppenheimer recruited top scientists, many of whom had fled Europe and Nazi Germany.

Oppenheimer's team gathered at Los Alamos, New Mexico, to decide on the design of the bomb. Work progressed rapidly, and in December 1944, Groves told Roosevelt that an untested bomb fueled by uranium-235 would be available in August 1945. A second bomb, fueled by plutonium, would need to be tested but would be completed by July 1945.

General Leslie Groves and scientist J. Robert Oppenheimer were in charge of the Manhattan Project.

Fueling the Atomic Bombs

The destructive power of atomic bombs results from the fission, or splitting, of certain atoms. The atoms that begin the nuclear reaction when they split come from an element called uranium-235. Scientists working on the first nuclear bomb had to separate uranium-235 from a more common type of uranium. Although they devised four ways to isolate uranium-235, none were certain or easy.

A second fuel that could create a nuclear reaction was plutonium, an artificial element that had been discovered in 1941. Scientists did not know whether they could produce the large quantity of plutonium needed for a bomb. Even if they could, no one knew whether the plutonium would create an atomic explosion.

The Manhattan Project scientists developed atomic bombs of both types. A uranium-based bomb was used on Hiroshima and a plutonium-based bomb was used on Nagasaki.

Roosevelt died in April 1945, and Vice President Harry S. Truman became president. Truman did not know that scientists were developing an atomic bomb. After he was informed, he established a committee, called the Interim Committee, of U.S. leaders in education and industry to consider the implications and use of the new weapon.

The committee met in the spring of 1945. Members considered two issues: first, they discussed the best way to demonstrate the power of the bomb in order to force Japan to surrender; second,

Members of the Manhattan project developed the atomic bombs at the Los Alamos National Laboratory in New Mexico.

they discussed the effect the bomb would have on international politics, particularly relations between the United States and the Soviet Union.

The committee members eventually agreed that the bomb should be used without advance warning. They concluded that the best target would be a city with a large war plant closely surrounded by employees' houses. One rationale for using the bomb was to destroy Japan's ability to wage war. Another rationale was to frighten the Japanese people and government with the power of the atomic bomb. Committee members hoped that this fear would lead Japan to surrender unconditionally.

The Interim Committee spent much of its time discussing the second issue: what impact the atomic bomb would

70   The War at Home: Japan during World War II

have on Soviet and American relations. By the spring of 1945, when the war in Europe was ending, the Soviet Union had dominated Poland. This greatly concerned the Allies. In addition, at the Yalta Conference in February 1945, Soviet leader Josef Stalin had told Roosevelt and British prime minister Winston Churchill that the Soviet Union would enter the war against Japan within three months after a European victory. The unconditional surrender of Germany was signed on May 7, 1945. As of June 1945, the Soviet Union had not declared war against Japan.

The choice the committee faced was whether to share information with the Soviet Union about building the atomic bomb or move ahead in secret so that the United States could remain the lead nation in nuclear weaponry. The committee decided on the latter. This decision marked the beginning of the nuclear arms race that dominated relations between the Soviet Union and the United States after World War II.

Truman was meeting with Churchill and Stalin when he was informed that there had been a successful atomic bomb test in New Mexico. There are conflicting reports as to just what Truman's thoughts were about targeting military or civilian populations in Japan. According to historians, no document exists that records

In 1945, President Truman defended his decision to drop atomic bombs on Japan by saying it had ended the war quickly and saved the lives of many U.S. troops.

Truman's decision to use the atomic bomb. He did not request position papers from his staff or engage in conversation about the advantages and disadvantages of using the weapon. Truman was concerned with ending the war in Asia quickly, however, and wanted to establish the United States as a strong opponent to the Soviet Union.

Scientists and the Bombs

A number of Manhattan Project scientists opposed the Interim Committee's decision not to share any information about the atomic bomb with the Soviet Union. They believed that this secrecy would result in a nuclear arms race. Through late spring and the summer of 1945, these scientists continued to ask U.S. officials to share information with the Soviets and to use the bomb only after giving Japan every opportunity to surrender.

Leo Szilard, the group's leader, was one of the scientists who had worked to create the world's first nuclear chain reaction. Born in Hungary, Szilard had fled the Nazis and, in 1937, immigrated to the United States. He had encouraged Einstein to alert Roosevelt about the Germans' advances in nuclear research. As Szilard worked on the Manhattan Project and the Allies were defeating Germany, however, he had second thoughts. He wrote in a memorandum dated March 4, 1944: "Initially we were strongly motivated to produce the bomb because we feared the Germans would

WAR DEPARTMENT

OFFICE OF THE CHIEF OF STAFF

WASHINGTON 25, D. C.

25 July 1945

TO: General Carl Spaatz
Commanding General
United States Army Strategic Air Forces

1. The 509 Composite Group, 20th Air Force will deliver its first special bomb as soon as weather will permit visual bombing after about 3 August 1945 on one of the targets: Hiroshima, Kokura, Niigata and Nagasaki. To carry military and civilian scientific personnel from the War Department to observe and record the effects of the explosion of the bomb, additional aircraft will accompany the airplane carrying the bomb. The observing planes will stay several miles distant from the point of impact of the bomb.

2. Additional bombs will be delivered on the above targets as soon as made ready by the project staff. Further instructions will be issued concerning targets other than those listed above.

3. Dissemination of any and all information concerning the use of the weapon against Japan is reserved to the Secretary of War and the President of the United States. No communiques on the subject or releases of information will be issued by Commanders in the field without specific prior authority. Any news stories will be sent to the War Department for special clearance.

4. The foregoing directive is issued to you by direction and with the approval of the Secretary of War and of the Chief of Staff, USA. It is desired that you personally deliver one copy of this directive to General MacArthur and one copy to Admiral Nimitz for their information.

THOS. T. HANDY
General, G.S.C.
Acting Chief of Staff

Incl # 1

get ahead of us and the only way to prevent them from dropping bombs on us was to have bombs in readiness ourselves. But now, with the war won, it was not clear what we were working for."[73]

Scientists tested the plutonium-based bomb on July 16, 1945, in New Mexico. The next day, Szilard sent a petition to Truman signed by sixty-nine members of the Manhattan Project. In the petition, scientists urged that the atomic bomb not be used against Japan unless officials spelled out surrender terms in advance. If Japanese leaders still refused to surrender and U.S. leaders had to use the bomb, the scientists asked that it be used only on unpopulated military targets.

The group stated in the petition that using the atomic bomb would usher in a new and dangerous era of weaponry: "If after this war a situation is allowed to develop in the world which permits rival powers to be in uncontrolled possession of these new means of destruction, the cities of the United States as well as the cities of other nations will be in continuous danger of sudden annihilation."[74]

For some reason, Truman did not receive the petition, and Manhattan Project leaders effectively silenced the opinions of the scientists who were against using the atomic bomb except as a last resort. After the war, Szilard worked to outlaw nuclear weapons and advocated the use of nuclear energy only for peaceful objectives.

The president's order to drop the bombs

Mass Destruction

On August 6, 1945, a U.S. B-29 bomber dropped an atomic bomb on the Japanese city of Hiroshima. On August 9, a B-29 dropped an atomic bomb on Nagasaki. Each bomb was about 9 feet (3m) in length, 2 feet (0.7m) in diameter, and weighed about 4.4 tons (4t).

The atomic bombs differed from conventional bombs. They were much more destructive upon explosion, and they sent radiation into the environment. At the moment of detonation, these weapons released three destructive energies: heat, radiation, and blast. First, the bombs emitted radiation and a fierce heat, which then generated a superhot fireball with temperatures reaching 12,632°F (7,000°C). The sudden rise in temperature expanded the air faster than the speed of sound. Following this air was a tremendous blast. The explosive force was equal to 13,000 tons (11,793t) of TNT in a conventional bomb.

As the blast spread, air pressure near the detonation site instantly plummeted from high to low. The air blowing out from the center reversed direction, and wind swept back in toward the center with tremendous force. Negative pressure increased the damage caused by the blast. Glass splintered into tiny fragments that pierced skin. Buildings collapsed into rubble.

After the explosions, large mushroom-shaped clouds hovered over Hiroshima and Nagasaki. When the clouds drifted, they rained a black material on the areas in their paths. The material contained

mud, dust, soot, and radioactive particles stirred up by the explosions. This black rain exposed even more people to radiation sickness.

According to the Hiroshima Peace Memorial Museum, an estimated 140,000 people in Hiroshima died by the end of December 1945. Approximately 70,000 people in Nagasaki died. The explosion killed many immediately. More died later from radiation sickness that they developed after the bombing.

In Japan, people who had been exposed to the atomic bombs were called *hibakusha*. Yamoka Michiko was a hibakusha. She was fifteen years old and worked as an operator at a telephone exchange in Hiroshima. By 1945, most Japanese students had work assignments to help in the war effort. On the morning of August 6, Yamoka says, she heard the B-29s as she walked to work:

I wasn't particularly afraid when the B-29s flew overhead. ... I put my right hand above my eyes and looked up to see if I could spot them. The sun was dazzling. That was the moment. There was no sound. I felt something strong. It was terribly intense. I felt colors. It wasn't heat. You can't really say it was yellow, and it wasn't blue. At that moment I thought I would be the only one who would die.[75]

When the atomic bombs exploded over Hiroshima on August 6th and Nagasaki on August 9th, 1945, the temperature beneath them was about 7,000 degrees, Fahrenheit (3,871 degrees Celsius).

Harmful radiation left behind by the atomic bombs has continued to make people in Hiroshima and Nagasaki suffer. Radiation can cause many injuries, including cancer.

After the blast, Yamoka lay under stone rubble. She heard others crying for help. "It was then I realized I wasn't the only one. I couldn't really see around me. I tried to say something, but my voice wouldn't come out."[76]

Like thousands of people in Hiroshima and Nagasaki, Yamoka was badly burned. In the chaos that followed the bombing, however, the only treatment for her burns was tempura oil. She was bedridden for one year. Without money, she received little medical help. Ten years after the bombing, Yamoka was in a group of hibakusha who were brought to the United States for medical treatment. She spent about a year and a half at Mount Sinai Hospital in New York. "I improved tremendously. I've now had thirty-seven operations, including efforts at skin grafts [skin transplant]."[77]

Koreans in Hiroshima

Many non-Japanese were among the victims in Hiroshima and Nagasaki. The number of dead is not clear, but an estimated 50,000 Koreans were in Hiroshima at the time of the bombing. About 30,000 of them died. Nearly all the remaining Korean survivors returned to Korea after it became independent in 1945.

During the war, Japan occupied Korea, and the Japanese wanted to make Korean culture similar to their own. For example, they instructed Koreans to change their names to Japanese names. Most of the teachers in Korean schools were Japanese and spoke only Japanese, which forced Korean students to learn that language. Many Japanese moved to Korea, and many Koreans moved to Japan. Shin Bok Su was a Korean who lived in Japan. She had married a Korean who was a subcontractor for Mitsubishi. During the war, Mitsubishi used Korean workers in Japan.

On the morning of August 6, 1945, Shin Bok Su and her husband were at home in Hiroshima with their three children and her husband's mother. Shin Bok Su had just started to wash the breakfast dishes. "Suddenly, 'PIKA!' a brilliant light and then 'DON!' a gigantic noise. I looked up. But I couldn't see anything. It was pitch black."[78]

After the explosion and the black rain, Shin Bok Su and her husband looked for

It is believed that around 30,000 Koreans who were living in Hiroshima were killed by the atomic bomb.

Hiroshima Peace Memorial Park

The Hiroshima Peace Memorial Park is more than 4 square miles (about 6.4 sq. km) of monuments and includes three buildings, one of which houses the Peace Memorial Museum. The park is in the Nakajima District of Hiroshima, where the atomic bomb directly exploded. This district had been a political, administrative, and commercial center of Hiroshima.

When the bomb dropped on August 6, 1945, thousands of volunteers and mobilized students were at work in the area, demolishing buildings to form a fire lane. Most of these people died in the explosion.

In 1949, officials enacted the Hiroshima Peace Memorial City Construction Law. They set aside the entire Nakajima District for peace memorial facilities. Each year, people attend an international peace conference held at the park.

The Hiroshima Peace Memorial Park was built to commemorate the victims of the atomic bomb, and to promote peace.

their children in the burning rubble. Soldiers insisted they flee the fires. When the couple returned the next day, the rubble had burned to ashes. Shin Bok Su's husband became ill from radiation poisoning and died. She explains that by the end of August, "we were living on the one rice ball a day they brought on a truck. … [A] neighbor told me that if you went to city hall, they'd give you money for the ones who'd died of the atomic bomb."[79]

Shin Bok Su went to the city hall and listed her family members who had died and their place of registration. She was told she was a foreigner. She recalls, "Until that moment I'd been Japanese. All I'd done was say my registration was in Korea."[80] She did not receive any support from the Japanese government.

Today a monument for Korean victims stands in the Hiroshima Peace Memorial Park. The monument's inscription reads, "The Korean victims were given no funerals or memorial services and their spirits hovered for years unable to pass on to heaven."

The Aftermath

After the bombing of Hiroshima on August 6, events moved quickly. On August 8, the Soviet Union invaded Manchuria. On August 9, they declared war on Japan. The fully supplied Soviet army outnumbered and crushed the badly weakened Japanese forces. The United States dropped a second atomic bomb, this time on the city of Nagasaki. Meanwhile, Japanese officials were deadlocked in their discussions about making an unconditional surrender.

Japan's leaders had a mixed response to the bombing of Hiroshima. Some claimed that the weapon had not been an atomic bomb and that the United States was spreading propaganda. Most historians believe, however, that the bombing ended any hesitation Emperor Hirohito felt about Japan's surrender.

The Japanese Supreme Council for the Direction of the War met on August 8—the day the Soviet Union declared war against Japan. The meeting ended in a deadlock. Hirohito and Prime Minister Suzuki were for surrender. They wanted only to retain the monarchy. Military leaders opposed that plan. In addition to retaining the monarchy, they wanted the United States to forego, or at least restrict, the occupation of Japan. They wanted Japan to be able to conduct its own war trials and disarming process.

As the council debated, an atomic bomb fell on Nagasaki. Those wanting to surrender feared an uprising against the government if the council could not agree on surrender terms.

The debate moved to the Japanese cabinet, where the military plan lost by a vote of thirteen to three. No action could occur, however, without a unanimous vote. At this point, Hirohito made an unusual move. He addressed the council and cabinet, stating his support for a surrender that would keep the monarchy in place. The emperor's address broke the deadlock.

On August 10, the Japanese government transmitted a message of surrender to Washington, D.C. Officials in the United States, after some consideration and discussion, saw this as a way to quickly end the war. They agreed that retaining the emperor would ease difficulties as they enforced Japan's surrender.

U.S. officials issued a carefully worded statement saying the United States would not remove the emperor immediately, but he would be subject to the authority of the U.S. supreme commander of the occupation forces. Furthermore, the final form of government in Japan would be established by the free will of the Japanese people.

On August 14, Japan surrendered to the United States. By August 18, all fighting in Manchuria ended. The official surrender papers were signed on September 2, 1945.

A Continuing Debate

Historians have often debated whether the United States needed to use atomic bombs against Japan. After the war, some U.S. military leaders stated that the

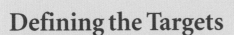

Defining the Targets

Truman announced the use of the atomic bombs to the American people in a radio speech on August 9, 1945. Truman had decided by the end of July to use the weapons against Japan. His definition of the targets, however, is unclear. He spoke of Hiroshima as a military objective, despite the fact that thousands of Japanese civilians lived there.

Truman wrote in his diary on July 25, 1945: "This weapon is to be used against Japan ... so that military objectives and soldiers and sailors are the target and not women and children."[1] He wrote that the target would be "a purely military one" and that the United States would issue a warning to the Japanese, urging them to surrender and save lives.[2]

In his August 9 radio address, Truman said, "The world will note that the first atomic bomb was dropped on Hiroshima, a military base."[3] He went on to state that the attack on Hiroshima was "only a warning of things to come."[4] He urged the Japanese people to leave industrial cities. By the time Truman made this statement, the United States had already dropped the second atomic bomb on Nagasaki.

[1]Truman quoted in Robert H. Ferrell, *Off the Record: The Private Papers of Harry S. Truman* (New York: Harper and Row, 1980), 55–56, http://www.dannen.com/decision/hstjl25.html. (accessed May 12, 2007)
[2]Ibid.

[3]Excerpt from *Public Papers of the Presidents of the United States: Harry S. Truman, Containing the Public Messages, Speeches and Statements of the President April 12 to December 31, 1945* (Washington, D.C.: United States Government Printing Office, 1961), 212, http://www.dannen.com/decision/hst-ag09.html. (accessed May 12, 2007).
[4]Ibid.

bombs might not have been necessary to end the war.

Some historians point out that there was growing opposition in Japan toward continuing the war. Even Truman noted in his personal diary on July 17, 1945, that Japan would most likely fall when the Soviets attacked. Soviet leader Josef Stalin told Truman that the Soviet Union would soon be at war against Japan. In response, Truman wrote, "He'll [Stalin] be in the Jap War on August 15th. Fini[sh] Japs when that comes about."[81]

At the time, U.S. officials worried that the Soviets were delaying a declaration of war against Japan. The perception was that the Soviets would declare war only as Japan was about to surrender, in order to reap territorial benefits such as Manchuria. Stalin, through Soviet spying, knew the United States had an atomic bomb nearly ready for use. He realized

These boys survived the atomic bomb blasts, but suffered serious radiation burns.

that the Soviet Union had to declare war on Japan quickly in order to gain Manchuria.

The debate over whether the United States should have used the atomic bomb will continue as more documents from the World War II years are released. Most historians agree, however, that using the atomic bomb against Japan ushered in a whole new era of international politics.

End of the War

Once the war ended, the Japanese faced

the enormous task of rebuilding Japan as well as building some semblance of relations with the Americans occupying their country. For years, Japanese people had been told that Americans were demons and barbarians. The Americans in Japan during the occupation tried to prove otherwise.

Sasaki Naokata was in elementary school when his class was evacuated from Tokyo to Miyagi in September 1944. He stayed at a small inn with his classmates. On August 14, 1945, when Japan surrendered, the students did their usual morning calisthenics at 6:00 AM. "We had no doubt that Japan's actions were just," Sasaki says. "We were convinced that the Americans and the British were demons. Not human beings. ... [We] shouted out to the exercises, Annihilate America and England! One-two-three-four!"[82]

After exercises, the students had breakfast and recited their allegiance to the emperor. They then went to work in a pumpkin garden they had planted. Later that day, students gathered to hear a special talk by Hirohito on the radio. The reception was so bad that they could not understand what he was saying. In the next day or two, they learned the war had ended, but they continued to shout their chant during exercises.

Sasaki remembers, "Our teachers told us, 'The war has ended.' They never said, 'Japan lost,' just that we could go back home." Some of Sasaki's classmates returned to Tokyo, but he was one of the students who stayed in Miyagi. The day the Americans arrived, he remembers that "we peeped out [of the inn windows] to try to catch a glimpse of them. What would they be like? Suddenly, it occurred to us, 'They must have horns!' We had images of glaring demons with horns sprouting from their heads."[83]

The students were in for a surprise, however, when the Americans gave out chocolates. Some of Sasaki's friends said that "'Americans, they're good people ... but I told them that couldn't be true. I swore that they must be lying."[84] Sasaki avoided meeting any Americans until he returned to Tokyo.

The U.S. occupation of Japan lasted seven years and introduced many new ideas about government, education, the economy, and the military to the Japanese people. Japan's culture became a blend of Japanese traditions and those new ideas.

Notes

Introduction: Japanese Daily Life, 1930-1945

1. Peter Duus, *Modern Japan*, 2nd ed. (Boston: Houghton Mifflin, 1998), 202.
2. Ibid., 210.

Chapter 1: Japan Goes to War

3. Haruko Taya Cook and Theodore F. Cook, *Japan at War: An Oral History* (New York: The New Press, 1992), 59.
4. Ibid.
5. Marius B. Jansen, *The Making of Modern Japan* (Cambridge, MA: The Belnap Press of Harvard University Press, 2000), 622.
6. Cook and Cook, *Japan at War*, 46.
7. Ibid., 45.
8. Quoted in Duus, *Modern Japan*, 224.
9. Ibid., 233.
10. Cook and Cook, *Japan at War*, 80.
11. Alvin D. Cox, "The Pacific War," in *The Cambridge History of Japan*, ed. Peter Duus (New York: Cambridge University Press, 1988), 334.

Chapter 2: The Emperor's Warriors

12. Cook and Cook, *Japan at War*, 122.
13. Ibid., 123.

14. Ibid., 124.
15. Meirion and Susie Harries, *Soldiers of the Sun: The Rise and Fall of the Imperial Japanese Army* (New York: Random House, 1991), 7.
16. Cook and Cook, *Japan at War*, 132.
17. Ibid., 132.
18. Ibid., 133.
19. Ibid., 106.
20. Ibid., 110.
21. Duus, *Modern Japan*, 240.
22. Cook and Cook, *Japan at War*, 263.
23. Ibid.
24. Ibid., 364.
25. Ibid., 264.
26. Ibid., 290.
27. Ibid., 342.
28. Ibid., 355.
29. Ibid., 356.
30. Ibid., 357.
31. Ibid., 360.
32. Emiko Ohnuki-Tierney, *Kamikaze Diaries* (Chicago: The University of Chicago Press, 2002), 1.
33. Cook and Cook, *Japan at War*, 321.
34. Ohnuki-Tierney, *Kamikaze Diaries*, 2.
35. Ibid., 85.
36. Ibid., 209.

Chapter 3: Promoting Loyalty

37. Herbert P. Bix, *Hirohito and the Mak-*

ing of Modern Japan (New York: Harper Collins, 2001), 427.

38. Ibid., 10.
39. Quoted in Cook and Cook, *Japan at War*, 339.
40. Thomas R. H. Havens, *Valley of Darkness: The Japanese People and World War Two* (Lanham, MD: University Press of America, Inc., 1986), 58.
41. Ibid.
42. Ibid., 67.
43. Cook and Cook, *Japan at War*, 253.
44. Ibid.
45. Ibid., 254.
46. Ibid.
47. Ibid., 255.
48. Quoted in John W. Dower, *War Without Mercy: Race and Power in the Pacific War* (New York: Pantheon Books, 1986), 207.
49. Ibid., 205.
50. Havens, *Valley of Darkness*, 62.
51. Quoted in Havens, *Valley of Darkness*, 66.
52. Cook and Cook, *Japan at War*, 205.
53. Ibid., 206.
54. Ibid., 207.
55. Ibid.

Chapter 4: The War at Home

56. Quoted in Havens, *Valley of Darkness*, 106.
57. Ibid., 108.
58. Cook and Cook, *Japan at War*, 177.
59. Ibid.
60. Quoted in Havens, *Valley of Darkness*, 87–88.
61. Ibid., 77.
62. Cook and Cook, *Japan at War*, 77.
63. Mikiso Hane, *Japan: A Historical Survey* (New York: Charles Scribner's Sons, 1972), 524.
64. Quoted in Bix, *Hirohito and the Making of Modern Japan*, 314.
65. Quoted in Havens, *Valley of Darkness*, 141.
66. Cook and Cook, *Japan at War*, 188–189.
67. Ibid., 189.
68. Quoted in Havens, *Valley of Darkness*, 165.
69. Hane, *Japan: A Historical Survey*, 545.
70. Cook and Cook, *Japan at War*, 345.
71. Ibid., 177.
72. Duus, *Modern Japan*, 245.

Chapter 5: The Atomic Bombs

73. Quoted in William Lanouette and Bela Silard, *Genius in the Shadows: A Biography of Leo Szilard* (New York: Charles Scribner's Sons, 1992), 259.
74. A Petition to the President of the United States, U.S. National Archives, Record Group 77, Records of the Chief of Engineers, Manhattan Engineer District, Harrison-Bundy File, folder number 76, http://www.dannen.com/decision/45-07-17.html (accessed May 10, 2007).
75. Cook and Cook, *Japan at War*, 385.
76. Ibid.
77. Ibid., 387.
78. Ibid., 389.
79. Ibid., 391.
80. Ibid.

81. Quoted in William Burr, ed., "The Atomic Bomb and the End of World War II: A Collection of Primary Sources," *National Security Archive Electronic Briefing Book No. 162,* National Security Archive, http:// www.gwu.edu/~nsarchiv/NSAEBB/ NSAEBB162/index.htm. (accessed May 12, 2007).

82. Cook and Cook, *Japan at War,* 468.

83. Ibid., 469.

84. Ibid.

For Further Reading

Books

Thomas B. Allen. *Remember Pearl Harbor: American and Japanese Survivors Tell Their Stories*. Washington, D.C.: National Geographic Society, 2001. American and Japanese survivors of the Pearl Harbor attacks describe the events surrounding the day the United States entered World War II.

Eleanor Coerr and Ronald Himler. *Sadako and the Thousand Paper Cranes*. New York: Putnam Juvenile, 1999. This true story describes Hiroshima-born Sadako and her battle with the "atombomb disease," leukemia. Inspired by a legend, Sadako sets out to fold one thousand paper cranes in hopes that she will be made well again.

Michael L. Cooper. *Fighting for Honor: Japanese Americans and World War II*. Boston: Clarion Books, 2000. Learn about the lives of Japanese Americans during World War II as they are forced into internment camps and as they serve in the U.S. military.

John Hersey. *Hiroshima*. New York: Vintage, 1989. This book is based on firsthand accounts from the people living in Hiroshima at the time the atomic bomb was dropped on their city.

Tomiko Higa and Dorothy Britton. *The Girl with the White Flag*. New York: Oxford University Press, 2003. This book tells of Higa's experiences as a seven-year-old when she wandered through war-torn Okinawa in 1945.

Jeanne Houston and James D. Houston. *Farewell to Manzanar: A True Story of Japanese American Experience During and After the World War II Internment.* New York: Laurel Leaf, 1983. Follow seven-year-old Jeanne as she and her family are forced to live in Japanese American internment camps in the wake of the Pearl Harbor bombings.

Linda Sue Park. *When My Name Was Keoko*. New York: Yearling, 2004. This book tells the story of a Korean brother and sister living under Japanese rule during World War II.

Kappa Senoh and John Bester. *A Boy Called H: A Childhood in Wartime Japan*. Tokyo: Kodansha International, 2003. This memoir of a young boy's childhood in Kobe before and during World War II describes the disturbing atmosphere of wartime Japan.

Yukio Tsuchiya and Ted Lewin. *Faithful Elephants: A True Story of Animals, People and War*. Boston: Houghton Mifflin, 1988. A zookeeper narrates this story about how the bombings of Tokyo affected the animals in the Tokyo Zoo.

Films

Empire of the Sun, DVD. Directed by Steven Spielberg, 1987. Burbank, CA: Warner Home Video, 2001. A British boy living with his family in China is captured by the Japanese and sent to a prisoner-of-war camp. His fascination with airplanes leads him to form a bond with a young Japanese pilot stationed at a neighboring air base.

Grave of the Fireflies, DVD. Directed by Isao Takahata, 1988. New York: Central Park Media, 2004. Two Japanese children struggle for survival after their mother is killed during the Tokyo fire bombings.

Internet

Thomas B. Allen. "Return to Midway." *nationalgeographic.com.*

http://www.nationalgeographic.com/midway/.

Track the progress of deep-sea explorers searching for the wreck of the *USS Yorktown,* which sank at the Battle of Midway. Then visit Mission Command to learn more about the expedition and the historic battle.

Hiroshima Peace Memorial Museum. *Hiroshima Peace Site.*

http://www.pcf.city.hiroshima.jp/index_e2.html.

Explore the Hiroshima Peace Memorial Museum located in Japan. Take a virtual tour, learn about the Peace Declaration, or read about the historical events leading up to the museum's founding.

japan-guide.com. *4 Monate Krieg [Months of War], Shanghai 1937: Photographs of Karl Kengelbacher.* http:// www.japan-guide.com/a/shanghai/index.html.

This collection of photos by Swiss photographer Karl Kengelbacher paints a vivid picture of the Japanese occupation of Shanghai, China.

John Parshall. *Imperial Japanese Navy Page.* http://www.combinedfleet.com.

This individual's site, devoted to the Japanese imperial navy, discusses the ships, submarines, and strategies of the Japanese navy during World War II.

Time Inc. "Hiroshima: August 6, 1945." Photo essay. *Time.com,* 2005.

http://www.time.com/time/covers/20050801/photoessay/.

Compiled by *Time* magazine to commemorate the 60th anniversary of the bombing of Hirsohima, this collection of photographs shows the effects of the atomic bomb on the people of Hiroshima.

U.S. Department of the Interior. National Park Service. *USS Arizona National Memorial, Hawaii.* http://www. nps.gov/usar/.

Explore the USS *Arizona* memorial in Hawaii. View photographs and learn about the history and significance of the memorial at Pearl Harbor.

Works Consulted

Books

Michael A. Barnhart. *Japan Prepares for Total War: The Search for Economic Security, 1919–1941.* Ithaca, NY: Cornell University Press, 1987.

W. G. Beasley. *Japanese Imperialism 1894–1945.* New York: Clarendon Press, 1987.

Herbert P. Bix. *Hirohito and the Making of Modern Japan.* New York: HarperCollins Publisher, 2001.

Iris Chang. *The Rape of Nanking: The Forgotten Holocaust of World War II.* New York: Basic Books, 1997.

Haruko Taya Cook and Theodore F. Cook. *Japan at War: An Oral History.* New York: The New Press, 1992.

John W. Dower. *War Without Mercy: Race and Power in the Pacific War.* New York: Pantheon Books, 1986.

Peter Duus. *Modern Japan,* 2nd ed., Boston: Houghton Mifflin Company, 1998.

Andrew Gordon. *A Modern History of Japan.* New York: Oxford University Press, 2003.

John Whitney Hall, ed. *The Cambridge History of Japan, Volume 6: The Twentieth Century.* New York: Cambridge University Press, 1988.

Mikiso Hane. Japan: *A Historical Survey.* New York: Charles Scribner's Sons, 1972.

Meirion and Susie Harries. *Soldiers of the Sun: The Rise and Fall of the Imperial Japanese Army.* New York: Random House, 1991.

Thomas R. H. Havens. *Valley of Darkness: The Japanese People and World War Two.* Lanham, MD: University Press of America, 1986.

Sabura? Ienaga. *The Pacific War, World War II and the Japanese 1931–1945.* New York: Pantheon Books, 1978.

Marius B. Jansen. *The Making of Modern Japan.* Cambridge, MA: The Belnap Press of Harvard University Press, 2000.

William Lanouette with Bela Silard. *Genius in the Shadows: A Biography of Leo Szilard, the Man Behind the Bomb.* New York: Charles Scribner's Sons, 1992.

Robert James Maddox. *Weapons for Victory: The Hiroshima Decision Fifty Years Later.* Columbia, MO: University of Missouri Press, 1995.

James L. McClain. *Japan: A Modern History.* New York: W.W. Norton & Company, 2002.

Emiko Ohnuki-Tierney. *Kamikaze Diaries.* Chicago: The University of Chicago Press, 2002.

Harold Stevenson, Hiroshi Azuma, Kenji Hakuta, eds. *Child Development and Education in Japan.* New York: W.H.

Freeman and Company, 1986.

Ronald Takaki. *Hiroshima: Why America Dropped the Atomic Bomb.* New York: Little, Brown and Company, 1995.

John Toland. *The Rising Sun: The Decline and Fall of the Japanese Empire, 1936–1945.* New York: Random House, 2003.

J. Samuel Walker. *Prompt & Utter Destruction: Truman and the Use of Atomic Bombs Against Japan.* Chapel Hill: The University of North Carolina Press, 1997.

Spencer R. Weart and Gertrud Weiss Szilard, eds. *Leo Szilard: His Version of the Facts, Selected Recollections and Correspondence.* Cambridge, MA: MIT Press, 1978.

Internet Sources

William Burr, ed. "The Atomic Bomb and the End of World War II: A Collection of Primary Sources." *National Security Archive Electronic Briefing Book No. 162.* National Security Archive. http://www.gwu.edu/~nsarchiv/NSAEBB/NSAEBB162/index.htm (accessed May 10, 2007).

Luke Colasurdo. "The Internment of Japanese Americans as reported by Seattle Area Weekly Newspapers." Seattle Civil Rights and Labor History Project. http://depts. washington.edu/ civilr/news_colasurdo.htm (accessed April 2, 2007).

Hiroshima Peace Memorial Museum. *Hiroshima Peace Site.* http://www. pcf. city.hiroshima.jp/index_e2.html (accessed May 11, 2007).

William Lanouette. "The Scientists' Petition: A Forgotten Wartime Protest." *Atomic Heritage Foundation.* http://www.atomicheritage.org/petition.htm (accessed May 10, 2007).

National Asian American Telecommunications Association. "Exploring the Japanese American Internment through Film & the Internet." http://www.asianamericanmedia.org/jainternment/ (accessed April 2, 2007).

A Petition to the President of the United States. U.S. National Archives, Record Group 77. Records of the Chief of Engineers, Manhattan Engineer District. Harrison-Bundy File, folder number 76. http://www.dannen.com/ decision/45-07-17.html (accessed May 10, 2007).

"Their Best Way to Show Loyalty (March 6, 1942)." *San Francisco News*, Internment of San Francisco Japanese, The Virtual Museum of the City of San Francisco. http://www.sfmuseum.org/hist8/editorial1.html (accessed April 2, 2007).

Index

Picture Credits

Cover photo: Hulton Archive/Getty Images

AFP/Getty Images, 27, 76, 80

Kaz Chiba/Photonica/Getty Images, 40

Getty Images, 68, 70, 77

Hulton Archive/Getty Images, 14, 15, 20, 25, 31, 32, 37, 52, 56, 58, 61, 63, 65, 75

Time & Life Pictures/Getty Images, 10, 17, 23, 34, 35, 39, 42, 59, 64, 67, 72, 74

Tohoku Color Agency/Getty Images, 54

About the Author

Linda Spencer is a writer, editor, and researcher of history textbooks, reference books, and trade books. She is a contributor to the African American National Biography project of the Du Bois Institute at Harvard University and a writer and editor of an urban social studies series.

About the Consultant

Dr. Christopher Gerteis is an assistant professor of East Asian History at Creighton University in Omaha, Nebraska.